Sufi Inayat Khan was born in Baroda, India, into a family of musicians. After establishing himself at an early age as a master musician, he worked for the revival of interest in the spiritual heritage of Indian music. He received initiation from his Sufi teacher and trained in the four major Indian schools of Sufism: Chishti, Naqshibandi, Qadiri, and Suhrawardi. When his training was completed, he left India for the West, where he lectured and traveled throughout Europe and America and founded the International Sufi Movement. His writings have touched the lives of many who welcome the breadth and wholeness of his vision, and who are inspired by his respect for every human ideal.

Education
from Before Birth
to Maturity

INAYAT KHAN

Sufi Publishing
An imprint of Hunter House Publishers

Reprinted from
The Sufi Message of Hazrat Inayat Khan

First published by Barrie & Rockliff, 1962

Second publication by
Sufi Publishing Company, Ltd., 1974

This edition published by Hunter House Inc.

© 1989, 1974, 1962 International Headquarters
of the Sufi Movement
Geneva, Switzerland
Cover design and special setting for this edition
© 1989 Hunter House Inc., Publishers
PO Box 847, Claremont, CA 91711, U.S.A.
All rights reserved

Library of Congress Catalog Card Number 89-81471
ISBN 0-89793-063-0

Cover design by Virginia M. Fontana

9 8 7 6 5 4 3 2 1   Fourth edition

Contents

1. The Education of the Infant 1
2. The Education of the Baby 25
3. The Education of the Child 46
4. The Education of Youth 71
5. The Education of Children 81
6. The Training of Youth 100

1
The Education
of the Infant

I T I S never too soon in the life of a child for it to receive education. The soul of an infant is like a photographic plate which has never been exposed before, and whatever impression falls on that photographic plate covers it; no other impressions which come afterwards have the same effect. Therefore when the parents or guardians lose the opportunity of impressing an infant in its early childhood they lose the greatest opportunity.

In the Orient there is a superstition that an undesirable person must not be allowed to come near an infant. If the parents or relatives see that a certain person should not be in the presence of an infant, that person is avoided, for the very reason that the infant is like a photographic plate. The soul is negative, fully responsive, and susceptible to every influence; and the first impression that falls on a soul takes root in it.

In the first place an infant brings with it to the earth the spirit with which it is impressed from the angelic spheres and from the plane of the jinn; it has also inherited from the earth qualities of both its parents and of their families. After coming on earth the first impression that an infant receives is from the environment, the surroundings, from those who touch it and move and work in its surroundings; and the impression after coming to the earth is so strong that very often it erases the impressions that an infant has inherited from the higher spheres, and also the heritage from its

parents. This happens because the mind that has been formed of the impressions which the infant has brought from the higher spheres is not yet positive. It is just like a pot of clay which has not yet gone through the fire; it has not yet developed.

The qualities that an infant has inherited from its parents are also in the same negative state; and they are perfected after the child has come on earth. Therefore the first impression that falls upon an infant after coming on earth is all the stronger. The first process in making pottery is to mould pots of clay, and the second process is to put them in the fire. When they are put in the fire they become strong, they become positive; before they are put in the fire they are negative.

In the same way a photographic plate is first negative; afterwards, when it has undergone a certain process, it becomes positive. And that is the process through which the soul passes in its infancy; it then goes through a certain development. All that it has brought from the higher spheres and from its family becomes developed, becomes positive or solid, in other words it becomes condensed; because that is the time when the spirit is being formed and is becoming positive. If an undesirable impression has fallen upon an infant at that time, no matter what education is given later that first impression remains concrete and solid. Nothing can erase it because infancy is the moment when the soul is becoming positive.

In educating the child the first rule that must be remembered is that one person must educate it, not everybody in the family. It is a great mistake when everyone in the family tries to train the infant or to take care of it, because that keeps an infant from forming a character. Each one has his own influence and each influence is different from the other. But most often what happens is that the parents never think of education at all in infancy. They think that is the age when the child is a doll, a toy; that everyone can handle it and play with it. They do not think that it is the most

important moment in the soul's life; that never again will that opportunity come for a soul to develop.

Should the father or the mother educate the child? A man's life demands all his attention in his work; the mother is born with the sense of duty towards her child, and therefore the mother has the first right to educate it. The mother can also quiet the child in the first days of its life, because the child is a part of the mother, and therefore the rhythm of the mother's spirit is akin to the rhythm of the child's spirit. The soul that has come from above is received and is reared and taken care of by the mother; and therefore the mother is its best friend. If there is anything that the father can do, it is to help the mother or the guardian to educate the child. If the child in its infancy were given entirely into the hand of the father, there would be little hope that it would come out right; because a man is a child all his life, and the help that is needed in the life of an infant is that of the mother. Nevertheless, later in the life of a child there comes a time when the father's influence is equally needed; but that time is not in infancy. As the Brahmin says, the first Guru is the mother, the second Guru is the father, and the third Guru is the teacher.

That one person who takes an infant in hand in order to train it must first establish a friendship with it. There was in India a Madzub, a sage, who used to live among elephants. He used to share his bread with them and sleep near them. At the same time there were those who were appointed to take care of the elephants. They controlled them with their spears and with their commands. Very often the elephants listened to them; but when an elephant was mad it would not listen, and often a keeper was killed at such times. The elephant would not recognize the keeper when it was mad. But this sage had a friendship with all the elephants, with the mad and the sober and with every one of them. He used to go near them and pat them and look at them and talk with them, and he would sleep near them unconcerned;

yet they would never touch him.

What does this show? It shows that there are two ways of controlling. One is the way of mastering, and the other is of becoming friends. By mastering you will diminish the will of the person you master; by being friends you will sustain his will-power, and at the same time help. In the one case you make of the person a slave; in the other case you make out of that person a king. In training an infant one must remember that his mind-power, which means will-power, must not be diminished, and yet an infant must be controlled.

There are five different subjects in which an infant must be trained in the first year: discipline, balance, concentration, ethics, and relaxation.

When once friendship is established with an infant the guardian is able to attract its attention and the infant will respond to the guardian. And that must be the necessary first condition; that condition must first be produced before beginning education. When once an infant begins to respond fully to the guardian, then discipline can be taught; but not by anger, not by agitation, as the guardian very often does; for an infant is often very trying, and is sometimes more stubborn than any grown-up person can be, and most difficult to control.

The best way of teaching the infant discipline is without agitation, without showing any temper or annoyance, only repeating the action before it. For instance, the infant wants something which it should not have, while the guardian wishes that it should play with a particular toy. This toy must be given continually into its hand; and when the child throws it away, or when it cries, give it again; and when the child does not look at it, give it again. By repeating the same action you will bring the infant automatically to respond to you and to obey. It is a wrong method when the guardian wishes to control an infant and wishes to teach it discipline by forcing a certain action upon it. It is

repetition which will bring about discipline. It only requires patience. For instance, if the infant is crying for its food or for something else when it is not the time for it, one should attract its attention towards something else, even against its wishes. The best thing is repetition.

Balance can be taught to an infant by bringing its rhythm at the moment when it is excited by a certain action, to a normal condition. For instance, when an infant is very excited, then the rhythm of its action and movement is not normal. By clapping the hands, or by rattling, or by knocking on something one can make the rhythm of the infant change to one's own rhythm; because any noise will attract an infant, and a noise made in a certain rhythm will influence its rhythm according to it. However excited the infant may be, begin by making some noise in its rhythm, and then bring it to a normal rhythm. For instance, if a rattle or something similar is first moved with the infant's rhythm, and then moved gradually in a slower rhythm, the infant will come naturally to that rhythm. The excitement will abate; the whole condition of the infant's mind, the blood circulation, the movements, the expression, everything will change to a normal rhythm.

There are three rhythms. There is a rhythm of passiveness, where the child is not active at all. That means the child is not well or there is something wrong with it, something that should not be. There is a second rhythm where the child is active but not excited; that is the normal rhythm. And there is a third rhythm where the child is excited. That excitement must be brought to the second rhythm, where the child was active but not excited. This can be brought about by giving a child what it likes. If it does not like one toy, give another toy; and if not that toy, another toy, and yet another toy. In this way do everything to occupy its mind, so that for some moments it will keep to one thing.

The excitement of an infant is the changing of the rhythm;

for the infant has no control over its own rhythm. It goes on at a greater and greater speed, until it cries or laughs. And the laughter or the cry is just the same. On the one side the infant will laugh and on the other side cry, because its rhythm is not normal. It can only be brought to a normal condition by the guardian's effort. But if one gets agitated or does not like the infant or is displeased with it, then one cannot help it.

Should one stop an infant from crying? It is better to distract the mind of a child that is crying than to let it cry, but at the same time it is very natural for a child to cry sometimes. If the child does not cry, it means that there is something lacking in it, that the child is not normal. One must use discretion in how much one allows the child to cry and when to stop it. One can allow it to go as far as a certain rhythm; when it has reached that rhythm, then it must not cry any longer; that is the time to stop it. But when a mother, annoyed with the infant, stops its crying the moment it begins, it has a bad effect on its nervous system. And very often a guardian will put the child into the cradle or somewhere else to cry by itself. But that means leaving it in the same rhythm, and that does not help. In that way the child will become worse and worse, and more and more nervous every day.

And now regarding the concentration of an infant. Toys with different colours, fruits, flowers, things that attract an infant should be brought before it, whatever attracts most; and then one must try and attract its attention to that particular object, let it play with it, let it look at it, be interested in it. In this way the guardian can develop in the child the faculty of concentration, which will be of the greatest importance when it is grown-up. If this quality is not developed, it will be very difficult for the child to concentrate when it grows up. Besides that, one brings a great interest into the life of the child when it begins to concentrate. And the child concentrates without knowing it. Give it any beautiful thing it likes to amuse itself with, and if its fancy is

taken by it, if it is absorbed in it, the child will concentrate naturally upon it. It is good for the child, for its soul and its body, because concentration is all the power there is.

Regarding ethics: this important word is used here, but in reality, the greatest ethics or morals that one can learn in life are friendliness, which culminates in generosity; and it is never too soon to cultivate this seed of morals in the child. When you give something to an infant which it likes, and with friendliness and sympathy and love you ask the child to give it to you, that brings about the feeling of giving and at the same time the feeling of friendliness. Very often the infant is not willing to give, but that means it is not trained to do so. You do not need to force it out of its hands, but by having patience and repeating your wish that the object may be given you, in the end the infant will give it. It may be that the first three or four times, if the child is very tenacious by nature, it will refuse, but in the end it will give it to you; and in this way it is taught the essence of morals.

Should one teach an infant that there are certain things it owns and other things which do not belong to it? Whatever an infant sees, whoever it belongs to, the infant owns it, and owns it as its birthright. It has not yet awakened to this world of limitations, of divisions. All that is there belongs to it; it really belongs to the infant. It is our consciousness of duality that makes us poor. The infant is rich, richer than anyone in this whole world. The infant has the riches of God; because, as everything belongs to God, so, too, everything belongs to an infant. And therefore there is no desire on the part of an infant to own anything: the infant owns all things. It is experience of the world that gives the child, as it grows, the desire to own, because then it becomes limited; then there are things which belong to others and certain things which belong to the child, and this means limitation.

Sometimes people think, 'Is it not wrong in a way to make a person generous in this wicked world, where everyone wishes to snatch away everything from everybody he sees? And especially all the simple people who are giving, who are generous, they are the ones who do not take, but others do.' The answer is that a selfish person is his own enemy. He thinks that selfishness is profitable, but his own action works against him. It might seemingly give him success. By selfishness he might earn riches or by a tenacious quality hold on to position, rank or something else; but at the same time he is defeating his own object, he is making himself weak. Besides in the end, whatever be one's experience, one will come to the realization that from those who pursue the world, the world runs away, and those who turn their backs on the world, the world follows. The spirit of all morals and ethics is friendliness, learning to sacrifice and learning to serve; and that last lesson can be given first to an infant.

Finally we come to relaxation. The infant can become very troublesome to the guardian and to others if it has not learned relaxation properly. But relaxation is learned by an infant much sooner than by a grown-up person. One only needs to put the infant in an even rhythm, to give it calm and quiet surroundings, to place it in a comfortable position, to make passes over the child to give its nervous system rest, looking into its eyes with sympathy and with the thought of its going to sleep, producing by one's own thought and feeling and atmosphere a restful and peaceful atmosphere for an infant so that it can experience relaxation.

It is very necessary for these five different subjects to be taught in infancy. Besides that, regularity should be observed in everything concerning an infant. In its food, in its sleep, in everything there must be regularity, because nature is rhythmic. The four seasons come regularly; the rising and the setting of the sun, and the waxing and the waning of the moon, all show that nature is rhythmic. By observing the rules of regularity with an infant one can build a foundation for a soul to grow up most successfully.

While the infant is being nursed by its own mother the heart quality is being formed in it; and it is upon that quality that the feeling of the infant depends for its whole life. Not understanding this, people today have other methods of feeding an infant; and by these that spirit of heritage and many merits and qualities that the child has to develop, become blunted. Mechanical food is prepared, and the child's heart becomes mechanical when it grows up. Once a Moghul emperor was very much astonished when he saw his son shaken by the noise of a gun, and he said to his minister, 'I cannot understand how a child of my family could show such a trait.' The wise minister said, 'If you will enquire how the child was brought up, you will find that it was not nursed by its mother.'

Just as the flesh of different animals is affected by each particular animal's character, so with everything one eats one partakes of its spirit. An infant is destined to receive qualities from its mother, in the form of food; and it is these qualities which become a fertilizer for the development of its heart. Food, made from the juice of fruits or meat and stored in bottles or tins, when given to an infant at an early age, forms undesirable atoms, and causes the infant to grow denser every day. If the mother is unable to nurse the infant herself, the best way is to find a nurse. And that nurse must be considered not only from the health point of view, as many do, but also from the character point of view. She must be looked at from every angle.

When the infant is cutting its teeth the mind develops; that is the time of the development of the mind. By keenly watching an infant grow, one will find that the day when it begins to cut its teeth the expression of its eyes changes; a mind is born, a thought is created. It is from that time that it begins to take notice of things and begins to think. The coming of the teeth is only an outward manifestation; the inner process is that the mind is forming. It is therefore a most important time in the life of an infant. For what is mind? Mind is the world. The infant at that time is forming the world in which it will live.

The moment when an infant begins to stand up and walk is the moment when power is beginning to become manifest in it. Enthusiasm, courage, the power of enduring, the power of patience, the power of perseverance, all these come at that time; it is the time when power is bestowed upon an infant. And the moment when the infant begins to speak is the time that its spirit has formed, that the mind is connected with the soul and connected with the body; the whole spirit is made at that moment.

From that moment the child should be considered as an individual. It is a little individual which then begins to have in itself the essence of everything and all things in the world; for in every soul there is a spark of every object and every quality that exists in the whole universe. And so, at this time when the spirit is completed, the essence of all the different qualities and merits and objects that exist in the world has formed as a spark in the infant.

The best way, therefore, for a mother to educate an infant is to educate herself. The calmness, the quietness, the tenderness, the gentleness, everything the mother cultivates in her nature at that particular time when the infant is nursed, the infant will receive as a lesson in its cradle. The heart qualities are the most profound qualities man has; brain qualities come afterwards; and it is the heart qualities which make the basis of the whole life. At that particular time such qualities as kindness, sympathy, affection, tenderness, gentleness, mildness develop, and it is at that time also that regularity is taught to the child, when the child learns its first lesson in being punctual. Unconsciously, it learns a rhythm. It knows the time when it should be fed. It does not need a watch to look at; it knows its time of resting, it knows its time of feeding. And by introducing rhythm into the mind of the child you put it on the road to perfection.

Mothers who get annoyed with an infant, who put it aside and say, 'Well, let him cry for a time', considering other work more

important, do not know what they are missing. Handling the child is the greatest opportunity. And even if they do it at the greatest sacrifice it is worth while; because once an infant is impressed with being neglected by the mother, there remains all its life an impression, in the deepest depth of its being, of a soreness; and when a person grows up he feels it unconsciously, and then he is displeased and dissatisfied with everybody he meets. When one lets an infant be fed at any time and be put to sleep at any time, that keeps it from a proper, even rhythm, and hinders its progress in life. For infancy is the first step on the path of progress.

When the mind of an infant is being formed, when it is cutting its teeth, people sometimes give it a rattle or something of rubber or wood, to put in its mouth. From a psychological point of view this is most undesirable, because it does not answer the purpose of the mouth. The mouth is for eating. Physically it is not good for its nerves and its gums, and psychologically it accomplishes no purpose. In the same way anything that is given to an infant at that age which does not serve a particular purpose, is a wrong thing to give. A child must not be deceived, even from his childhood, by an object which has no purpose. Even from infancy every object that is given to the child must inspire him with its use. An object that has no use, that serves no purpose, hinders the progress of an infant.

The moment when the infant stands up and walks is a moment which should be guarded with the greatest interest and keenness. This is the moment when the powers are being manifested; and if these powers are used and directed towards something, a box or a tray, or something which is not inspiring, which does not give back something to the child, those powers are being blunted at every effort the child makes to go towards it. Then the best thing is to call the child towards oneself, to gain the child's sympathy and attention. This attracts the child and gives new life.

Nothing one does with an infant should be purposeless. If it is so, then its whole life will be purposeless. There are many who after they are grown-up cannot accomplish a certain purpose in their life. Very often the reason is that from their childhood, when the forces were rising, they were not directed to a purpose. It does not matter if a sweet were put there, or a fruit or a flower; if the child was directed to bring that, then there is a purpose. But when the child is directed to go to a box, or to the wall or door, where it has no gain, then the effort which has risen unconsciously is lost.

The beginning of a person's life is of greater importance than the latter part, because it is in childhood that the road is made for him to go forward in life. And who makes the road? It is the guardian of the child who makes the road for it. If that road is not made and the guardian is asleep, then the child has great difficulty when it is grown-up. School education and college education will come afterwards; but the education of the greatest importance in the life of a soul comes in its infancy.

Now there is a symbolism in the actions of a child. If the child goes straight towards something, that shows the straightness of his nature. If the child is wobbly, then it shows lack of will-power. If the child goes to one side and stands there, and then goes to another side and another, and then walks back, this shows that there is a fear, a doubt, and that the mind is not clear. If its mind were clear, the child would go straight. If it stops on the way, then this itself is a hindrance in its future life.

If the child runs and reaches a certain place, it is impulsive and venturesome; it will jump into something when it is grown-up. But if an infant as soon as it begins to walk adopts a proper rhythm and reaches a desired spot, that infant is very promising. It shows singleness of purpose and balance by the rhythm of its walk. An infant which is beginning to walk, and which does not look at the guardian, but is only interested in what it sees before

it, will be indifferent when it is grown-up; but an infant who after going to a place is attracted again to the guardian shows the heart quality. He will be a loving soul.

Should one do gymnastics with an infant? No, an infant is too young for gymnastics. But every action that can be taught in order to bring about a rhythm and balance and discipline, and concentration and affectionate feeling, works towards building its future; and thus the first education is the foundation of its character.

By saying that one person and not several should train an infant, one does not mean that the infant should be kept away from everyone. No doubt others can entertain the infant for a moment; they can see it, they can admire, they can love it; but only for a short time. If four or five persons are handling it at the same time, then the child's character will not be decided; it will neither be one thing nor the other. If the same guardian watches over the child all the time this will always be beneficial whether the infant is with others or not.

When an infant reaches the age of two or three years, it is most beneficial if it is taught a moment of silence. But one might say, 'How can a silence be taught?' A silence can be taught by attracting an infant's attention very keenly, and this can be done by rhythm. When you make a certain noise by clapping your hands or by making a rhythm, and when you attract the attention of an infant fully, then if you wish it to be inactive, you can hold it in an inactive condition for a moment; and that can do a great deal of good. It could become a kind of religious or esoteric education from infancy. If an infant can keep his eyes from blinking, and his breath and the movement of his hands and legs suspended for one moment, it accomplishes even at that age a meditation.

Furthermore, when the infant is beginning to utter sounds, such as *ba, pa, ma, boo, goo*, one should not take it as something unimportant or something which has no meaning; one must realize that each such sound is a new lesson that an infant has learnt from the world, and one should give that word great importance, because it is the first word and that is a divine word. The best way of training an infant to learn the meaning of these words and sounds is to repeat with it the same sounds, to let the child hear the same word over and over again, and become interested in what it is saying; and then to attract its attention to objects and persons of that name. It is in this way that the words *ma* and *pa* have come into being. It is not that someone else has given these names; the infant has given them to its father and mother. Others have added to those words and made them mater, mader, mother, but it began with *ma* and *pa*. It is a natural word, it has come from the depth of the mind of the infant; it is a divine word. Its origin is a divine origin.

Such a word as 'mummy' is the third word, and is brought about with the help of the guardian. The first word is *ma*, the second word is *mama*, and the third word is *mummy*; *mama* is extended to *mummy*. As fashions come in dress, so there come fancies in words. People like to use a certain word for some time and then it becomes a fashion.

One can help an infant by repeating different words with it and by pointing out to it the meaning of the words, instead of always urging upon it another word to be repeated. One spoils the ear of an infant in that way. The Nawab of Rampur once expressed a desire to the chief musician of his court to learn music himself, and the master said, 'I will teach you music on one condition, and that is that you do not listen to every kind of music that comes your way. When bad music is heard the ear becomes spoiled; and then you cannot discriminate between bad music and good music.'

So it is with an infant. The infant is saying *pa*, and the mother is saying *leaf*. The infant is saying something, and the guardian is saying something else. There is no harmony and no purpose is accomplished. The infant is unable to say *leaf*; it is beginning to say *pa*. Its own intuition has guided it, and it is better to go with nature and to let an infant be enlightened by every sound it makes, by showing it something connected with that sound. It is in this way that an infant is helped to speak. Then, if it learns to speak by nature's method, it promises one day to speak from intuition.

It is the will that has brought the child to the earth, otherwise it would not have come. It comes by its own will and it stays by its own will. The will is like the steam that makes the engine go forward. If the child wishes to go back, that depends upon its wish. It is always by the will of the soul. And therefore in the child you see the will in the form in which it has come. But often during childhood the will is broken, and then it remains broken all through life. If in childhood the parents took good care that the will was not broken, then the will would manifest itself in wonders. The child would do wonderful things in life if its will was sustained, if it was cherished.

The infant that is born on earth brings with it the air of heaven. In its expression, in its smiles, even in its cry you hear the melody of the heavens. The Sufi point of view is that an infant is an exile from heaven, and that is why its first expression on earth is a cry. The soul that comes from above feels uncomfortable on the dense earth. This atmosphere is strange and not free; and it is a feeling of exile that makes the soul cry, a feeling of horror, of a terror of this world of woes.

When a child comes to the earth without a cry it indicates abnormality. The child is quite abnormal, and it will not have a full development, because the new sphere has not struck it; in other words, it is not fully awake to the new sphere. Bring a waking person here, he will look at what is going on; bring a drunken person, he will sit here in intoxication. He does not know what is going on, he is not aware of the conditions, he does not care. And so it is with an infant. There is hardly a case where an infant does not cry; but if there is such a case there is something wrong. Why is the soul so much attracted to the earth? It is attracted to the earth because it is bound to the earth. It is the soul's passion to manifest; it is only expressing its passion.

Before the infant came to the world it had educators too, one or many educators. It first had educators on the jinn plane, the inhabitants of that plane and the ones going back who met it on the jinn plane. The older ones on the angelic plane have their experience, their life, their feeling to impart to a new soul going further on the journey. It is from there that an infant has brought the feeling of admiration for all beauty, the feeling and love of harmony, innocence, and the depth of feelings. Then it met other teachers on the jinn plane, and these teachers are the ones to whom it was directed from the angelic plane; because according to its association on the angelic plane it takes a certain route, a certain direction. It is the first instructors in the life of an infant who have the influence which directs and determines its destiny on the jinn plane.

Can the soul choose its instructor on the angelic and jinn planes, one may ask, or is it helpless before anyone who is attracted to it? There is always free will and the lack of it on all planes. If we go into the midst of the city, there are some things that we purposely want to see; we are looking for them. At the same time there are many things which attract our attention also without any intention on our part. In the same way, when the soul arrives it is attracted to things and beings which it had no intention of being attracted to, and at the same time it has its choice; it has both.

The experiences of the infant before birth on the higher planes are not directed by the stars as we understand it from the astrological point of view; it is from the time that it comes to the earth that its connection with the stars begins. But at the same time

there are other factors which to a large extent determine the soul's destiny.

On the jinn plane the soul receives instruction from the inhabitants of that sphere, and also from those who have just returned from the earth, eager to give to the infant their experience, their knowledge, and all they still have with them brought from the earth. They would have given to it even what they had on the earthly plane, but no one is allowed to take to the other sphere what he has collected here. All that belongs to this sphere a person must leave behind in order to be free and in order to be allowed to enter the higher spheres. And therefore, what they have is what they have collected in those spheres while they were on earth. That is all they have, the thoughts, impressions, feelings, experiences, knowledge that they have gained. It is all, so to speak, a collection which a person makes in the higher spheres, but it is not something which can be deposited in the bank. So when man has left to the earth all that he has borrowed from the earth, then he goes on with only that property which he has deposited or collected in the higher spheres without knowing it. Very few on earth know that while they live on the earthly plane they are collecting something in the higher plane. They live at the same time on the higher plane, but they do not know it.

With this heritage and with this knowledge and instruction that it has received from one or many, an infant comes to the earth. People might object that an infant does not show any sign of any knowledge of the earth nor of the heavens; it does not show any sign of the angelic world nor of the world of the jinns. They do not know that an infant can perceive or can receive impressions of human beings much more readily than grown-up people. The infant at once senses the right person; and sometimes it perceives more than a grown-up person. Besides that, we grown-up people think that we appreciate music, but if we realized the sense that an infant has brought with it of appreciating sound and rhythm, we would never boast of knowing music. The infant is music itself. In the cradle it is moving its little arms and legs in a certain rhythm. And when our music falls on the ears of an infant it is of the lowest character compared with the music it is accustomed to.

At the same time it begins to move its legs and its arms to the rhythm of the dense music. We may believe we have the finest music, but for an infant it is the most dense music; it is accustomed to much finer music than we can conceive. It longs for it, it looks for it; and what we give as a substitute does not satisfy it. For a moment it tries to listen to it, it tries to enjoy, to like it; but at the same time it does not feel at home, it turns its back and wants to go away. Only for a moment it tries to enjoy it, thinking it is something that belongs to its country, which means the heavens; and then it finds out: no, it is foreign. That is the only reason why an infant will cry in the middle of a concert; if it were not so an infant would enjoy it more than anyone.

It takes some time for an infant to become accustomed to the life of the earth. And what makes it accustomed to it? Colour. Colour is what attracts most, and then sound. When it gets accustomed to the dense sound and the dense colour, then it gradually begins to lose its heavenly attributes. And when its first wish is to change from being an angel and walk like an animal, when it begins to creep, it begins its earthly life; but before that it was an angel. Infancy is angelic; it is not the jinn time, it is the angelic time.

Infancy may be divided into three parts: the first three years are real infancy. The first year the infant is most angelic; the second year there is a little shade of the jinn sphere; and the third year it begins to manifest the earthly influence, the influence of this world. So an infant becomes worldly in its third year.

Why is it that an infant, though still conscious of the angelic

planes, has no feeling of kindness originally? The angels are not obliged to be kind. They are kindness itself, but that angelic kindness must awaken here. Kindness and cruelty are learned after coming here; when the infant comes, it comes with love alone. Everything else is taught here. And if the guardians knew this, they would help the child much better. There are many qualities that the soul has brought from the higher spheres, but those qualities remain undeveloped if they remain buried, if they are not given an opportunity to develop. Thus, if kindness has not been given an opportunity to develop in the child, the kindness will remain buried in the depth of its heart all its life, and it will not know it.

Parents sometimes think that it is bad manners for an infant to put its hand in its mouth, and therefore they give it something made of wood or rubber, or something else. It very much hinders its real progress in life, because every soul is born to reach the ideal of being self-sufficient. An infant tries from the beginning to put its hand in its mouth when the mouth wants something; and the parents, in order to teach good manners, give it something else, making the infant more artificial. If they left it to its natural tendency, they would help its growth, its progress towards a higher ideal. What are the saints and sages and adepts and mystics doing during their time of spiritual attainment? They eliminate everything in their life which makes them depend on things outside. They eat with their hands; instead of taking plates they use leaves; and everything they do shows that they wish to become independent.

By independence is meant self-sufficiency: that what they can get from their own self they must not look for outside. That is the principal motive of those who are striving for self-attainment, because it is the means of overcoming the sorrows and troubles and woes of this life. One sees a constant striving in the life of the adepts to make themselves independent of outside things as much as possible. On the other hand worldly people think it progress if they can become daily more dependent on others. Every step we take is towards dependence; and the more we depend upon others, the more we think we are progressing. In the end we come to such a stage that for what the soul needs, what the mind needs, what the body needs, we depend upon others. And, not knowing this, we teach the child to put something else instead of its little hand in its mouth. In reality, it is natural for an infant to put its hand in its mouth; and that is the purest and the cleanest toy that it can have to play with.

The Qur'an says there is a time for everything. And so there is a time, there is a day, an hour, a moment fixed for the child to change its attitude: to learn to sit, to learn to stand, to learn to walk. But when the parents, eager to see the child stand or sit or walk, help it, the child will do it before the time, and that works against its development; because it is not only that it begins to learn to sit or to stand or to walk; there is a far greater meaning in it. These are different stages which an infant goes through in its spiritual life. Physically these are just ordinary actions; spiritually it is a stage. When the child sits it is a stage; when it stands it is a stage; when it begins to walk it is a stage. These are like three first initiations in the life of an infant.

In order to understand the meaning of an infant's laughter and cry one must become an infant, because it is the language of another sphere. But when a person does not trouble about it, then its cry is only a nuisance and its laughter is a game. Sometimes people wish to make the child laugh more and more because they are interested or as an entertainment; or people neglect the child, leaving it to cry, and pay no attention; or when an infant is crying the mother says, 'Be quiet, be quiet'; in all these cases they lose the opportunity of understanding the language of an infant. This is the opportunity for the guardian, for the mother, for the one who looks after an infant, to learn the heavenly language. For there is nothing that has no meaning, and every movement of an infant, who is an expression, an example, from above, has a meaning. But as we are absorbed from morning to evening in the responsibilities and duties of the world, we forget the responsibility and duty to the infant. And because the infant cannot speak in our language and tell us how neglectful we are of what it wants, and what it needs, and what can be done for it, there remains a wall of separation between mother and child.

An infant knows and feels the presence of an undesirable person in the atmosphere around it. It is very unwise when people engage any nurse that comes along to take care of their infant. And it is unfortunate in these days when mothers have many other occupations, that they cannot take charge of their infant themselves, and have to send it to what they call a crèche, a place where they take care of infants. This does not mean that to keep an infant among many other infants is not right, but at the same time it is only after we have grown up in this dense world that we come together, if not very much, at least partially. It is always difficult for many people to work together, to be together, to live together; and yet we have been here on this earth so many years, and we have become accustomed to the life of the earth. But what about an infant who has just arrived and who is placed among other infants, where the gap between the evolution of one infant and another is infinitely greater than the difference between two grown-up persons? They are not yet accustomed to being together, and the atmosphere of one infant is bad for another. It is all right for many soldiers to be together in one room, for many patients to be together in one hospital; but for many infants to be put in one place after being exiled from paradise to this earth, imagine what it means for them to have this experience! It is like a king banished from his kingdom. No doubt after six months or a year an infant becomes accustomed to it; but at the same time the individuality of the soul and the development of the personality become blunted.

No doubt a great amount of patience is required to take care of an infant. But patience is never wasted; patience is a process through which a soul passes and becomes precious. Souls who have risen above the world's limitations and sorrows, the world's falseness and deception, they are the souls who have passed through patience. If it is the destiny of the guardian or the mother to acquire patience, she must know that there is nothing lost, but that she has gained something in her life. To raise an infant, to look after it, to educate it, and to give oneself to its service, is as much and as good a work as the work of an adept; because an adept forgets himself by meditation, a mother forgets herself by giving her life to the child.

There is always a possibility of giving an infant bad habits. For example sometimes a guardian enjoys the laughter of an infant and thus makes it laugh more and more, because it is amusing. But however much an infant has laughed, so much it must cry afterwards, in order to make a balance. And then there may be another mother who, as soon as an infant has opened its mouth to cry, says, 'Quiet, quiet!'; but if an infant then becomes quiet, something in its character is broken. It wants to cry, it must be allowed to cry; there is something in its character that wants to come out.

There is also a tendency in an infant to throw things about, to slap, to kick, to tear, to break things. Sometimes it is such a little thing that is broken or spoiled that the mother thinks its behaviour is enjoyable. But if an infant is allowed to do what ought not to be encouraged, it will only make it difficult for it later. It must be corrected, but at the same time it must not be corrected with anger or annoyance. It should be corrected repeatedly by giving the infant something to do which is different from what it was doing before. One should always keep an infant focused on things that will be good for it, and try to divert its attention from things that it must not do, instead of enjoying and amusing oneself with things that it does which the parents may think do not matter.

It is very difficult to stop an infant in its first year from destroying things. Besides the inclination to destroy things is a great virtue in the child. It is the desire of the soul to know the mystery of life; because every object before an infant is a cover over the mystery the soul is looking for. It is annoyed with it because it is a cover. It wants to know, by breaking it, what it is.

However, it is possible to stop the infant from breaking things, but by suggestion, not by getting annoyed. Annoyance must be avoided, because it is not good for an infant if one is annoyed with it. The more patience one has with an infant the better; its will becomes more powerful. But if you are annoyed, then the nervous system of the infant deteriorates, and it becomes depressed. Its nervous system becomes contracted, it becomes tired; and when it is grown-up a fear remains. One must be extremely careful with an infant that its nerves do not get cramped. Its nervous centres are delicate; and these are the centres which are intuitive centres. Later on, these centres will help the soul to perceive higher knowledge. And if these centres become cramped by the annoyance of the guardians, then the infant has lost that faculty by which it should grow and profit in life. The infant will understand; one must have patience. One should repeat, 'You must not break it', every time he breaks something. Let him break ten times, and every time just say, 'You must not break it'; that helps.

Regarding the bad nature of an infant, sometimes it shows stubbornness and obstinacy even to the extent that one feels annoyed and begins to scold it. But that is not right. Scolding has a bad effect on the nerves of an infant. And once a bad effect has been made on the nerves of an infant there will be a mark of annoyance on the nerves all through its life. The best thing at such moments is to call the attention of the infant repeatedly to something that will take away that thought, and we must never tire of doing it. It is this which will make it come back to a proper rhythm.

There are two principal temperaments in infants: active and passive. There is an infant that is quite happy in the place where it is put, quite contented, enjoying itself; it cries only when it is hungry. And there is another infant who is always doing something; either it must cry, or break, or tear something; it must do something all the time. The best thing is to bring the infant back to a normal rhythm. An active infant must be quieted by the influence of the guardian; by attracting its mind to a certain thing, by beating time and getting it into a certain rhythm. Infancy is the time when the impulsive nature can be trained, and that is the time to draw out what is really best in the impulsive nature and utilize the impulsive nature to its best advantage.

When an infant is quiet, contented, passive, happy-natured, one must not be contented about it, because it may not prove to be good in the end. That infant should be made a little more active. A little more attention must be given to it, a few more playthings, a little more thought must be given. It should be stimulated, it should be picked up and its attention attracted to this or that, so that it may become more active and more interested in the things it sees; that will bring about a proper balance.

2
The Education
of the Baby

IN THE first five years of a child's life, the first two years are considered as infancy, the next three years as babyhood. Very often there is a desire on the part of the guardians to educate the child of four or five years either in a kindergarten or at home. That time in the life of a child is a time of kingship, and the eagerness on the part of the guardians for the child's education to begin is only pressing it with our competitive life. For our life is competitive and it is getting worse and worse every day; and the same spirit unconsciously exerts pressure on the life of the child, urging it on to become one among the many competitors of the world, in order to guard its interest when it is grown-up. But what about the most blessed years that destiny has granted to the baby, when there is no worry, no anxiety, no malice, and no ambition? That is the real kingship. If you compare a baby with a king, you will see that the baby is the king and the king is the imitation.

No doubt it is better that the child learns in the kindergarten, where it is taught only the alphabet, than at school, because there its mind is distracted and it has something to play with. But at the same time, even attracting the mind of the child to a limited horizon is limiting the growth of its soul. It was much better to do as the peasants and the uncivilized people used to do, keeping their children at that age perfectly free to run about and to climb the trees and play with the soil, and to jump and run about and play with their playmates. It is a great mistake on the part of the guardians to deprive the child of that freedom and happiness which the heavens have granted it in that period.

The story of Adam's exile from the Garden of Eden shows that there is a certain time in a man's life when he is in the Garden of Eden, and after that time he is exiled from there and no longer experiences that joy and happiness and freedom that once the soul possessed. There is not one soul in this world who has not experienced the Garden of Eden, and that Garden of Eden is babyhood.

Now there comes the question of controlling children's intense activity. In the first place their intense activity is tiresome to other people in the family because their interests are different. But if its interest is different that is not a fault on the part of the child. For instance the guardian may be working or writing, or taking a rest, or thinking about something worldly, while the child is playing and making a noise; and the guardian thinks, 'No, this is wrong'. But wrong according to which law? It is a lack of consideration when the guardian is not tolerant of the activity of the baby. No doubt it does not always fit in with the earthly people. But babies are not earthly, they are heavenly creatures. They must be given the liberty to enjoy their heavenly life, just as we are entitled to experience the life of this earth.

No doubt there is a certain limit to it. One may say, 'We will not let them break the things in the house; we will not let them spoil things; we will not let them trouble us in our work'; but all that is earthly. In point of fact, the guardian has no right to prevent the baby from enjoying its free activity, and every effort must be made by the guardian to allow this. In the children's play, in their hustle and bustle, in their crying and jumping and running and climbing their soul is expressing itself. We call it naughty, but they do not consider it so. Even if it is called naughtiness they think it is lawful for them; and it is so. And because we control them and make them suit our own lives, their energy, their enthusiasm, their spirit become limited; and in this way their real progress is hampered.

At this age a child is conscious of the higher spheres. Many times children have known much more about what was going on at the front during the war than even the authorities knew. They knew intuitively, sometimes in their dreams, sometimes in a kind of deep imagination; and when they predicted something, that thing happened. And that shows that at four, five, six, and seven years the child is extremely intuitive, because at that time it is under the influence of the jinn.

At the age of three, four, and five the baby is very imitative; it likes to imitate everything it sees. And the best way of educating the baby is to bring before it everything that is worth imitating. For instance, sounds, notes, rhythm, and anything that is pertaining to tone and rhythm build and beautify the character, and form the foundation of character in babyhood. And it is best that till the age of five the baby should not be taught anything in the way of figures or alphabet or letters. Regularity is the only thing that can be taught to children at that age, and without their knowing it; regularity in sleeping, in waking up, in food, in playing, and in sitting quiet.

I was very much interested in what Madame Montessori told me when I was in Italy, that besides all the activities that she gives to the children, she makes them keep a silence; and after a little time they like it so much that they prefer silence to their activity. And it interested me still more to see a little girl of about six years of age who, when the time of silence came, went and closed the windows and closed the door, and put away all the things that she was playing with; and then she came and sat in her little chair and closed her eyes, and she did not open them for about three or four minutes. You could see on her innocent face an angelic expression. It seemed she preferred those five minutes silence to all the playing of the whole day. Children enjoy silence when they have become accustomed to it. Silence is not a strain on a child. Only in the beginning it might appear to be disagreeable to a child, who is eager to play and run about, to be sitting and closing its eyes. For children to sit and close their eyes seems hard in the beginning. But when they have had some silence every day for a week, they begin to enjoy the happiness of silence.

Sometimes there is a tendency on the part of the guardian or of those around a baby to enjoy its irritability. It is a kind of entertainment for them. Because they love the baby they are amused by the little gesture of annoyance on its part. But by appreciating it, by recognizing it, by observing it, they develop that characteristic. The best thing, however, would be to overlook it, not to acknowledge it, not to be conscious of it, not to feel for one moment that the child is irritable; because once the guardian takes no notice of it, that tendency of the baby will begin to decrease.

There is also a tendency on the part of the guardian to be annoyed at the irritability of the child. That too is wrong; because by being annoyed one gives to the baby, just like fuel to the fire, the energy to be more irritable. Guardianship of a baby requires great patience; and the more patient one is, the more wise one is with the baby, the more one can help its soul's progress.

Very often behind the irritability either of a child or of a grown-up person there is a hidden reason, and it may be a physical reason. There may be something physically wrong which others do not know of; and they only think that this child is irritable by nature. They attribute the irritability to the child, instead of seeing that there is something physically wrong with it. By trying to find out what it is, one will be able to tolerate that condition better.

There is another tendency in the baby, and that is that during its development it has varied moods. Some days it is loving, other days it is less loving; some days it is more angelic, other days it is less angelic; in this way it changes its moods. In this phase the greatest care should be taken that all such moods of the child are controlled, without forcing one's own will too much upon it. For instance, if the baby is very much inclined to cry, to laugh, to destroy things, or to play, the best thing is to direct its attention to something else. If it is laughing very much, one should direct its attention to something that will keep its mind busy, that will make it more balanced, and take its attention away from the idea that makes it laugh. If it is crying, the same thing may be done: to divert the child's attention from the object, the thought, or the condition which makes it cry, and in this way to bring about a balance in its life.

Is there any place in the life of a baby for religion? The answer is that the best opportunity to sow the seed of religion is in baby-hood, because it is at that time that the angelic quality is fresh and the jinn quality is beginning to develop. And in what way should one teach the child religion? The ancient lesson of the God-ideal, which all the prophets and teachers have given and which will always prove to be the best lesson there is, is to give the child the idea of God: God of goodness, God of beauty, God of compassion, God of love, God of harmony. If in any child there is a spiritual tendency, it will show even from the age of five years. Love for prayer for instance, love for the God-ideal; the feeling for something sacred, a reverence for something religious, it might seem that this was already there, that the child was born with it.

Sometimes the religious, devotional, and spiritual attributes are

distinctly seen in a child who is growing from infancy to child-hood. The spiritual tendency is inborn, and when it shows itself in a child one should know that the child has brought it from above. The child is very often more responsive to the God-ideal than a grown-up person; because the grown-up person, by being absorbed in the things of the world, has lost the idea of God. He has the world before him. The child has not yet the world before him; and therefore the child is more capable of conceiving the thought of God than a grown-up person. And if this opportunity is lost, then when they are grown-up they feel that something is missing in their life, and they think, 'If only I had known about God, it would have been much better.' But now it is too late; now it is difficult for them to conceive the thought of God, because the seed was not sown at the right time.

There are numberless souls who, because their parents have not given them the idea of God, find it most difficult to conceive it; and at the same time their soul is constantly seeking for it. But the guardian must be most careful that he does not sow the seed of bigotry with the religious ideal. If he does this, then a great harm is done to the child. By bigotry is meant this: first there is a time when a person believes in God, and that is a very blessed time; and when he is more evolved in the wordly life then he fights for his Church, that is then his main idea; and when he is still more evolved, then he despises other creeds. And so a person evolves higher and higher; it is that evolution which is called bigotry. If a child is impressed from its childhood by that spirit, then the main object is defeated. The main object of religion is to elevate the child to the higher ideal; and that can be done by giving it the key of religion, and that key is the God-ideal.

The guardian must also endeavour not to give the child heavier food than it can digest in the form of religion. Very often there are guardians filled with a philosophical idea, with a special idea of religion, with an ethical conception of religion, who wish to

inspire the child at that age. But in this way they do harm; because instead of giving the first lesson they have perhaps given a lesson which is too advanced for the child, and it is all lost. It is just like giving too much water to a growing plant which dies because of the flood of water that it cannot absorb. There are very many guardians who talk philosophically to a baby, because their philosophical conception is so overpowering that they think it must be poured out on the child; but if the child is too full of it, then it will only forget it. We must become children with the child in order to bring it up. We must speak in its own language, and we must only give it what it can understand.

Once a nurse came to me and said, 'This child asks wonderful questions, and I cannot answer them'. I said, 'What are the questions?' She replied, 'When this child was going to say its evening prayer before going to bed, it asked me, 'If God is in heaven, up in heaven, then why must I bow low to the earth?'' ' The nurse was very perplexed; she did not know how to answer; but if this child had not been answered, from that moment its belief would have gone, because that is the time when the soul is beginning to enquire into life and its mystery. I asked the child, 'What did you say?' The child explained it to me, and I said, 'Yes, God is in heaven, but where are His feet? On the earth. By bending towards the earth, you are touching His feet'. That gave it the explanation that although the head of God is in heaven, the feet of God are on the earth; and therefore touching the earth is touching the feet of God. It was quite satisfied.

Very often children are on the point of losing their belief because their belief is just like a young plant, a little seedling that comes out of the earth; and if this is not well guarded, it can be destroyed in a moment. Therefore one must be most careful. It does not matter if a grown-up person has a belief today and gives it up tomorrow. It does not matter because his belief was nothing. But a child's belief is different. A child's belief is something serious. It has no doubt; what it believes, it believes seriously; and therefore its belief is real belief. If that belief is destroyed it is a great pity and a great loss.

A child one day came to its guardian very perplexed because a boy had said to it, 'Do you believe in Santa Claus? If you do then it is not right, because there never was such a being as Santa Claus.' This child was very disappointed, because it had just written a letter to Santa Claus before Christmas. And in its great despair it came to the guardian to ask, 'Is it true that Santa Claus exists, or is it not true?' Now suppose the guardian had said, 'It is true', then in four or five years' time the child would have come and said, 'No, it is not true'; and if he had said, 'No, it is not true', then all the child's belief would have been totally destroyed. It would have been completely changed if the guardian had said, 'It is not true'. That would have rooted out, just by saying no, all the innocent religious belief from the heart of that child. But the guardian said to it, 'Remember, all that the mind can conceive exists. If it does not exist on the physical plane, it exists in the sphere of mind. So never say it does not exist. To the one who says that it does not exist, say that it exists in the sphere of mind'; and the child was very impressed by this answer.

A child can remember such an answer all its life. If the child evolved so that it could touch the heavens, it would still believe it. Never in life need it say, 'I do not believe it', and at the same time this is a belief that is tangible. It can never say, 'It does not exist, it is not real'. It can say, 'It is real', both as a child and as a grown-up person.

It is best to keep the child ignorant of all stories of ghosts as long as one can. Ghost stories impress a child and interest it very much, and by this its mind goes in another direction, a direction which is not suitable for it. The best thing is always to avoid conversation about ghosts and spirits, and also about the devil.

And the best way of avoiding it is to turn it into a joke. A witty answer that will turn the mind of the child from the idea of ghosts to a joke would be the best thing. But at the same time to say there is no such thing as a ghost or devil is taking upon oneself a very great responsibility; it is denying something which is written in the Bible and in other scriptures, and could make a child an unbeliever, so that when it grows up it will not believe in anything.

It is essential that in childhood a religious teaching be given. If the guardian is not able to discuss religion with the child, it is better not to try but to give the child the habit of sitting in silence for a moment, and thinking about the higher ideal, God.

The way of Christ was to give humanity the ideal of God, God as the heavenly Father. And what was the reason? The reason was that it is conceivable. Even a child can understand that idea: Father, heavenly Father, the real Father. Besides, all the different names that the prophets and teachers have given to God are really not appropriate; it was only to make people understand. Their minds could only conceive those names: the Judge, or the Creator, or the Supreme Being, or the King of the Day of Judgment. They are not the names of God; all names given are not the names of God. God cannot be limited to those names; they are too small for God. Yet at the same time it is the best one can do to make the ideal of God as concrete to the mind as possible. What strength, what a help it is for the child to think from early childhood that there is a Friend unknown, unseen; to be able to say, 'There is Someone who hears my prayers. Someone who in my troubles and difficulties can be with me, Someone whose blessing I ask, Someone who protects me, Someone who is like my mother and my father and yet unknown, unseen'. Even if the child is not able to make it clear to itself, yet unconsciously it will feel it like a support from within. It will feel that it can stand with that support, a support so great that at all times, whether the child has its parents or not, in all conditions it can feel, 'There is Someone who is always there with me'. And if this ideal is built from childhood by wise guardians, it helps the child for its whole life.

The guardian need not be discouraged to find obstinacy and temper and selfishness in the little child. He must know that either the baby has inherited it or it is the result of some defect in its physical health, and it must be treated most wisely. Fire is increased by fire, and the plant of temper is watered by anger. The more the guardian reacts, the more he will encourage that tendency in the baby. To become annoyed with the child who is in a temper is to fan the spark of anger in it. The best way is first to get the baby to respond to him, and then with that response to make it act according to the will of the guardian.

If the obstinacy of a baby can be directed to its own advantage, then it can be benefited by the obstinacy. Obstinacy can be very useful; for most of the great people in this world have become great by a certain obstinacy in their character, because obstinacy is a strength and a power in itself. An obstinate businessman can be successful, an obstinate warrior can win, an obstinate politician can accomplish his purpose, an obstinate industrialist can accomplish great things. Obstinacy, therefore, if rightly directed, can be of great use. One only needs to mould the mind of the child in such a direction that its obstinacy may become fruitful. It is the obstinate child who will sit and finish a task that is given to it; if it had not that obstinacy it would not do it. Sometimes from obstinacy comes the spirit of rivalry, and very often the spirit of rivalry becomes the means to success.

Manners are most important, and especially at four and five years of age the lessons of manners must be given. The first lesson to be taught is knowing when to come near and be loving, and when to sit quiet and obedient in the presence of the guardian.

If the guardian is showing affection to the baby all the time the baby becomes spoiled. There must be change. There must be a time when the child is loved; it requires love, love is its sustenance; but there is another time when the child must be obedient; it must sit or stand or do something that it is told to do; and at that time there is no display of tenderness.

There is one thing that must be taught from babyhood, and that is not to argue. If that tendency is not suppressed from babyhood, it will grow unconsciously perhaps and afterwards the guardian will find it most disagreeable. A person in whom this tendency is not checked from childhood will show insolence in some form or other, no matter how good the manners he learned afterwards. Also, if the child contradicts it should always be checked, even to the extent that the guardian may say to the child, 'As you are young you do not know enough. Even if to you it appears wrong, there is some right in it. You do not know and therefore you may not contradict; and you may not contradict your guardian before others. If you think that your guardians are wrong, when the others are gone you may come to your guardians and say, "That was not right, what you said"; but you may not say it before others, because you do not know enough about what your guardian has said. There may be some reason in it.' When you have said this to the baby once or twice or thrice it understands. A child is easier to work with than grown-up people.

At the same time the baby should be inspired with the spirit of self-respect. There may be something delicious on the table, something attractive in the room, something beautiful within its reach, there may be some gold and silver coins lying loose in its presence, but its natural tendency of taking them, of losing them, of breaking them, of spoiling them, must be checked. And how must it be checked? The baby must not think that it is forced to keep away from what attracts it, but it must feel that it is self-respect not to look at it; that it is glad to take its eyes away from the sweet that is on the table, that it feels a great pride and honour to think that it will not even look at it. That teaches the baby patience; and its self-respect gives it more joy than even the sweet and the toy would give it, because it touches its very being; it wakens the soul when the child feels pride in refusing something that in its heart it is attracted to. This does not mean that the baby should be denied all that is good and beautiful. No, it must be taught that when something is given, it can be accepted; but when it is not given, then the baby must be proud enough to control itself.

The child must be taught not to be over-enthusiastic about anything that appeals to it, whether it is a sweet, a toy, or something beautiful; it must be taught not to show too great an appreciation. Because it is a humiliation, it is making oneself small before the object that one is enthusiastic about. The baby must be too proud to be enthusiastic. And remember that a baby will begin to appreciate this, if not in the beginning, then a little later. Self-control gives the child such a feeling of power and satisfaction that it begins to enjoy it.

A child must be checked in the feeling, 'You have taken more than I', or 'My little brother, or my little sister, has received more than was given to me'. That must be stopped. It must not judge; it must appreciate it if the little brother or sister has got more; it must be glad. It will not be glad naturally, but if it is taught then it will be glad; it will enjoy being glad. Virtues are virtues because they give joy once they are practised. If a virtue does not give joy, it is not a virtue.

Very often guardians do not attach importance to what toys they give the baby to play with. There are certain toys which have the effect of making it lazy; there are certain toys which will make it confused, or which will bring about stupidity, or make the child irritable or timid. Unconsciously they have that effect upon the child. Besides, playing with certain toys does not bring any benefit. When we think that every moment of baby-hood is so precious in the life of the soul, and that this soul is to be denied something that can add to its progress, it seems a great pity.

There must be discrimination even in choosing toys, as to what toy will inspire the children and help them, and will elevate their souls. There are many meaningless toys with horrible faces, horrible toys with nothing beautiful about them. The child likes them because it likes anything. Sometimes a child likes a doll without arms or legs. But we must give the child toys which are finished and not without arms or legs.

Sometimes it likes horrible toys most. For instance, what does a teddy-bear do to the child? Does it inspire the child, does it elevate its soul? It does nothing. On the contrary, it gives to the receptive mind of the child the impression of an animal, which is not good. Very often there are toys which give no inspiration, which have no action, and therefore have a confusing effect upon the child. One gives the child a teddy-bear because one thinks that it likes it. But why must we give something to the child because the child likes it? A friendship with a bear!

There is much else to occupy one's mind. Besides, there are certain toys which give no exercise to the mind and no inspiration to the child, and that makes it lazy. Anything constructive is good. For instance, a train that runs, or an instrument that sounds, that is good for a child, or anything that it can construct with, as the pieces of a puzzle that a child can make a picture from, or the little bricks and pillars and different things from which it can make a house or something else; all such toys are good. In short every toy must be constructive, must lead to some purpose; that should be the guiding principle.

It is not very good for the child to play with animals. If the child can have a kind feeling towards the animal it is quite enough; because every association has its special effect on the child. And very often the tendency of the guardian is to think that the child likes the animal very much. That may be so, but it is not good for the child; from a psychological point of view it is sometimes bad for it.

Boys' toys should not be given to girls, neither should girls' toys be given to boys. If boys get accustomed to playing with the toys of girls, then their mind goes in another direction; and it is the same with girls. It is better that the girl has her own toys and the boy his own toys. Both must have toys appropriate for them, and very often guardians do not discriminate between them.

One may wonder if it is bad for children to play with tin soldiers. Yes, it is, because it develops a tendency towards fighting. But it is a delicate and very subtle question, and one must not lay down rules about it. What a terrible thing it would be if as a child a person did not play with bow and arrows and sword or anything that is soldier-like, and then when he was twenty-one years of age, the country called him to defend it and he knew nothing about warfare, for he had never received any preparation for it! And another question arises: when the whole nation is ready for war and there is one youth, perhaps, who feels, 'I will not go because I am not in agreement with the principle', it is his right to disagree with the principle, but at the same time he is willing to accept the order and peace that is maintained by the nation, to share all the privileges of being a member of the nation. He shares them, but he refuses what the majority wants him to do. It is against his principle certainly; but what the majority wishes him to do he refuses although he does not refuse the privileges. If he refuses the privileges also it is different. If he does like the sages, if he goes away from the country and stays in solitude under the shade of a tree, it is different. If he does not want money, if he says, 'I do not compete with you; I do not want to have any benefit from your progress in life; I do not keep any money that a thief can steal from me, for which I might then have to come to your court', then it is different. But if a person is ready to share all privileges that belong to the country, and then when the need of defence comes says, 'It is against my principle', that is quite another matter. Never think that this means standing up for war. But at the same time let the little boys be capable of everything.

Every little manner that is sweet in the child, every good little tendency it shows, should be emphasized and appreciated. One must not take it silently. Never think that by showing the child appreciation it will become conceited. No, the child will be encouraged. It will be just like watering a plant when you appreciate anything that is nice in the manner of a baby. And there is never a time in one's whole life when one appreciates a word of praise so much as when one is a baby. The child really appreciates it and is encouraged to do the same again.

Then there is the question of blame. When the child has done anything wrong, the first thing is to reason with it, to convince it. And if it is not convinced at once, then try a second time, and then a third, a fourth. Never be disappointed, even if one has to try ten times to convince the baby by argument.

Very often a guardian thinks it is too much waste of time to argue with a baby who does not understand; it is more easily done when one scolds and finishes with it. But that does not finish it. Much scolding blunts the spirit of the child. The spirit of the child must be kept so fine and so sharp that the slightest glance could make it feel hurt. But if one scolds the child all the time, it blunts its spirit, and the child becomes worse and worse.

Never for one moment imagine that the child will not take in your reasoning. If not the first time, it will take it in the second or the third time. One must continue to reason with the child;

and by doing so the guardian brings the child closer to his spirit, because the child feels a friendship between itself and the guardian. By reasoning one draws the child nearer to one's own spirit. And if the child does not listen to the reasoning and the guardian has reasoned for many days, then the next thing to try is temptation; to tempt it with a sweet, with a flower, with something that it likes, with love, with appreciation; to say, 'You have done right', 'Now you have done it nicely, and I will give you a toy,' 'I shall give you a sweet if you will do it'. Show appreciation, tempt it to do right. This is the next step. It is preferable that the child should learn with reasoning; but if not, then a reward must make it listen.

If even a reward is not enough, then the third way is scolding, punishment. But scolding must be short. The scolding must be in the voice, in the way it is said. It must not be hard, nor must it be harsh. There must be a certain tone that the child at once realizes is scolding. One must avoid scolding as much as one can, but if one cannot help it then that is the third way. There is a wrong method which guardians very often adopt, perhaps in the East more than in the West, and that is to frighten a child by saying some bogey is coming or something like that; if it continues to be naughty something will come to frighten it, a ghost or a spirit. That is the worst thing that one could do to a child, because every such shock takes away a great deal from the enthusiasm of its spirit to progress. It hampers the progress of the soul to be frightened by anything.

Very often a stubborn child who does not listen and who does not change, by being asked to turn around three times changes its point of view at once. If one wants to make the child feel more deeply, if one tells the proud child to go and stand in the corner with its back turned to everybody, it really feels hurt. One can also ask it to go out of the room and stand outside the door. That hurts the child still more.

Is it right to punish a child? Punishment is natural. Every soul is punished in some way or other. For everything one does there is a punishment; it is the law of nature. The law of life has punishment just the same. But punishment for the child must be gentle. It is better to avoid a severe punishment, but rather to give a little mental punishment, which makes the child realize that it is being punished. Suppose one told the child to go from one place to another five times or ten times; in point of fact, walking up and down can be an enjoyment for the child, but by the very fact that you have given it as a punishment the child does not like it. The feeling, 'I am punished', in itself corrects it. In order to punish you do not need to torture a child; you only need make it realize that it is being punished. That is quite enough.

Sometimes guardians think it is necessary to slap a child, to slap its face. Slapping is sometimes dangerous, because there are veins and delicate organs in the forehead and on the temples, and slapping could cause a condition which though not manifest at the time, might become so after twenty or forty years. And therefore instead of slapping it is far better to tweak the ears. Punishment has a very bad effect when it blunts the sharpness of the child's spirit. Very often punishment may work with the child, but in some way or other it blunts its fineness; and therefore one must try to do without it if one can. Then, after giving good advice and counsel and encouragement, and after showing appreciation and doing everything possible, the last thing is to tweak the ears.

Boys are sometimes more stubborn than girls; and if you give them a little punishment in the form of gymnastics it corrects them. If a boy is told to sit down and stand up fifty times, it helps him in his gymnastics, and at the same time he feels punished. Boys are difficult to control, and can easily become insolent if they are not trained from their babyhood. A girl by nature is thoughtful, and a boy by nature is the contrary. When a boy is thoughtful it means that life has taught him.

Very often both boys and girls can be taught by means of repetition. For instance, if you told the boy to repeat a hundred times, 'I will not make pencil marks on the wall', after repeating it for a hundred times he will be impressed by it. There is a great difference in the effect of making a child repeat a phrase and making him write the phrase a hundred times. If you make the child write the phrase a hundred times the effect is one quarter compared with the effect if you had made him say it a hundred times; that is the best punishment you could give him. While he is repeating a hundred times he becomes impatient, he becomes tired and he is displeased with it; at the same time he is impressed that he is being punished. When one asks a child to stand for a long time and repeat, 'I will not be mischievous', in fifteen minutes time it will take away a great deal of that spirit of mischievousness from it.

One may ask what one is to do if the child will not take the punishment, will not repeat a phrase, for instance. But the child will surely do it. If from babyhood it is not controlled, then it becomes insolent and refuses afterwards, but if from babyhood it is taught to obey a normal child will not refuse.

How should one treat a child when it is angry? By not partaking of its anger. That is the first principle. When the guardian loses his temper because of the child's anger, then everything goes wrong, because then there is a fire on both sides. The child is not helped in that way. It is best to keep calm and direct the child's attention to something else. If the child is in a temper and the guardian gives it a punishment, that does not do it any good. It is wasted.

There is, however, another time when the punishment may be usefully given. Punishment may be given when the child is in its balanced, normal condition. For instance, if you held a court in the house, where the children could be judged at a time when they had forgotten all about what they had done, then they would remember. That is the time when whatever punishment is given will have effect. But when the child is cross and the punishment is given immediately, it is lost. At that time every effort must be made to take away the temper by kindness, by sympathy. But very often that is where the guardian makes a mistake.

Must a child obey without understanding? There is a vast difference between the mentality and experience of the child and of the guardian. Very often the child will not know why it is told, 'You must not do it'; and if the child always asked, 'Why must I not do it?' then it would be difficult, because very often it cannot even be explained. And very often it had better not be explained; very often it is better that the child only listens to the guardian and does not argue. Just as the musicians in the orchestra are accustomed to look at the conductor's baton, so a baby must be taught to look at the glance of its guardian. And if the guardian is wise enough to conduct the action of the baby from morning till evening by his glance alone, he is sure to train that child to be a most promising soul in the future.

And now another question arises: how much must a baby be kept in control, and how much must it be allowed to play with its playmates? There must be certain times when the baby is allowed to play with its playmates. But the guardian must select them, because the association in childhood is more responsible for the baby's future than the association when grown-up. Very few people think about this. Mostly the tendency of the parents is to think that any child that comes along can play with their child. But when it comes to home education it is not the same thing; that system will not do; because home education is an individual education, while school education is different. There they are all together, but home education is something else, it is a different ideal. And this must be remembered, that school education without home education is not sufficient.

The greatest drawback today is that home education is lacking, and only school education is given. And therefore in many personalities there is something missing that ought to have come from home. If there were thousands of schools most wisely and wonderfully organized, they still could not take the place of home education. Home education is the foundation of school education; and that opportunity of being educated at home must not be denied to a child, because it is a great blessing.

There must be discrimination in regard to the playmates that one chooses for the baby. And the time must be limited so that the baby plays with its playmates during that time only. But if the child is allowed to run wild in play and there is no limit to it, then no training is given and it is not education. There is need for play, but only for a certain time and no longer.

Regularity in life is the rhythm of life; and the more the rhythm is maintained in life, the better it is. It is not necessary for many grown-up persons to handle a baby; it is better that only one handles it. It is just like an orchestra and its conductor. If there were four conductors directing the orchestra, they would spoil it. Even if there were four hundred musicians playing there must be only one conductor. It is the same thing with the guardian. If there is more than one person to guide the life of the child, it will be spoiled. In the case of the two parents one must become the hand of the other. But if both wish to manage their child, then it will be spoiled.

If the baby is an orphan, what can one do? That is destiny; one can only be sorry about it. And those who are blessed by Providence and who have to look after an orphan, should consider their responsibility as that of a parent, of a guardian towards the orphan that is in their charge. But every woman and every man in this world should consider it their duty, whenever they are in contact with a new soul, to be as parents to that soul. For in the total scheme of life all the elder ones have to take the part of the parents to the younger ones, while those have to take the part of the children to those who are older. So that we each have our older ones and our younger ones to look up to and to look after.

The greatest ideal that one can give a baby is to look up to its parents. That is the first ideal; and if at that time the baby has not received this ideal, then all his life he will have no ideal, because there will be no basis for it. Someone went to the Prophet Mohammad and said, 'Prophet, I am so spiritually inclined, and I would so much like to follow your Message and come and meditate in your presence. But I am still young and my parents need me at home. What shall I do?' The Prophet said, 'Remain at home first, because some consideration is due to your parents.' One might think that the Prophet was a greater ideal still; why did the Prophet deny him that ideal, why did he send him home? Because the Prophet thought that was the first ideal. If the youth did not reach the first ideal, how could he get to the second ideal? If he did not look up to his parents, did not appreciate them or feel grateful to them, how could he appreciate the Prophet?

It is the parents' duty to give that ideal of themselves to their own child. Not for their own sakes, but for the good of the child. That ideal must be given from babyhood so that the child looks up to its parents as it would look up to the King or Queen, or to God or to a prophet. When the ideal is sown in that way, in the child from the beginning, then it will flourish, and then that ideal will become a guiding torch in the life of the soul.

3
The Education
of the Child

WHEN the child is six years of age babyhood ends and child-hood begins. There are cases of earlier or later development, but as a rule the change comes at six or seven years. This is the age of great conflict because the soul is taking a new step forward in life. And this inner conflict very often seems troublesome to the guardian. The child is restless and obstinate, too active and less responsive. At the age of seven this ends and a new life begins. The child naturally becomes calmer, more harmonious, more responsive, and yields to any advice that the guardian would like to give.

Today many think that at six years old the child should go to school; but this is a mistaken idea. This is the time when the child should be at home, because six years is the time of conflict, and seven is the beginning of a new era for the child. If at that time the child misses home education and is sent to school to be trained with other children, that takes away the distinctive care which should be given to it at that age. If the child has once been sent to school, one should not take it away from the school; but at the same time it would be better if one could manage to keep the child from school and give it home education till it is nine years of age. But if the child would like to go to school should one not send it? One does not send the child to school for its pleasure; and also the guardian can give pleasure to the child by giving it the training which it likes at home. It is not necessary that the guardian should teach the child letters and figures at home. The earlier one teaches a child, the earlier his mentality will wear out in life; and if one does not teach him, it only means that when the mind is mature it will grasp more quickly. Just as the voice producer says that if you begin to sing at a certain age your voice will flourish, and if you sing before that age it is not good, so it is with the mentality of the child. If the child begins before its time, it only means that in the end the mind will wear out before its time.

Where there are many children in the house and the guardian cannot give all his attention to each, this means a little more responsibility; but at the same time it is easier too, because for the guardian with so many children at the same time there is a greater opportunity and greater practice.

What generally happens is that guardians become so tired taking care of the child that they feel a great burden lifted from their shoulders when the child goes to school, for then they feel comfortable, being quite free for six or eight hours, because one child in the house can be equal to one hundred children. Guardians think that they love the child, and very often they believe that they make all sacrifices; but at the same time when it comes to bearing with an energetic child in the house, then there is a doubt. It does not mean lack of love, but they think, 'I would be happier if the child were away for a while'. But they only think so because they do not know what a great opportunity it is to begin to train and to guide the child. It is an opportunity for its whole life; and if the guardian misses it, it means a loss to the child.

The reason why the guardians are anxious to send the child to school is that they are conscious of competitive life. They see how there is competition in business and industry and on all sides of life; and in order to train the child soon enough, so that it may take up life's duties and responsibilities, they wish to do it too early. The consequence is that the child has lost the best time it could have had at home; a time of rest and comfort, and freedom from all anxiety about the work that it has to do at school; so that its mind could have matured properly, and it could have begun the school work at the right time. It is because the generality of people are so competitive in every profession and business, that we make the coming generation suffer; we deprive the children of their freedom, of the time which they ought to have at home to play and to think little and enjoy life more, and to keep away from worries and anxieties. We take away that best time in the life of the child by sending it to school.

A proper rhythm should be given to the child in babyhood. This is the only training necessary, in order that it may be neither too excitable nor too lethargic; and that its interest may grow, and that, while playing, it may get familiar with nature and gain what knowledge nature can give. When a child is six years of age it is not able to grasp an ideal, and any ideal given to it at that age is wrong. Only evenness of rhythm should be maintained in the everyday life of the child. Its natural tendency is to laugh too much, to play too much. Everything that it is interested in it does more than it should do; and if the guardian can try to keep it normal and balanced it will make a great difference.

At the age of seven the child is ready to conceive any ideal given to it, because that is the beginning of childhood. And now comes the question: what ideal should be given? The first ideal should be the ideal of a respectful attitude towards its elders; because once grown-up without this ideal a soul never learns respect. He only learns the form, but it does not come from within. Among a hundred persons who are compelled to act respectfully there is perhaps one person who is respectful in spirit; ninety-nine persons are compelled by conventionality to act respectfully, and that action gives no joy. But when that attitude comes from within, then it comes with joy; it gives joy to others and it brings joy to oneself.

Today we see the general attitude of insolence increasing as time goes on. It is the outcome of negligence on the part of the guardians at the time when it should have been taken in hand. Many think that this attitude ought to be taught in school, but the school is not responsible for it. It belongs to home education, and it is the guardian who is responsible for it. And it is at this particular age of seven that it must be given. Of course if a child has not a respectful attitude, one can very easily accept it. One smiles at the lack of it. One thinks, 'It is a little child, what do you expect from it?' One's love and affection for the child make one think, 'Oh, what does it matter? Is it not a child?' But to take it like that is to work against its future. This is just the time when a respectful attitude must be developed. The tendency to argue, the tendency to hit back, the tendency to refuse, to disobey, the tendency to speak in a disagreeable tone, even the tendency to frown and make a disagreeable face, all these disrespectful tendencies grow with the years in childhood. One does not think that they are of any importance, but when they are allowed to grow they grow as enemies, bitter enemies of that child. And, as Sa'di says, Ba adab ba nasib, bi adab bi nasib, 'The one who has respect in him, he will be fortunate surely; and the one who lacks it will be unfortunate'.

The lack of this tendency is a misfortune for man. And besides the man who has no respect for another has no respect for himself. He cannot have it, he has not that sense. Self-respect only comes to the man who has respect for another; you will always find in a disrespectful person a lack of self-respect.

Another ideal is a regard for the guardian. By guardians are meant parents or those who take care of the child and take the place of the parents. And regard is not only respect, it is more than respect. It is the feeling that 'this is my guardian', a feeling that 'I owe him something', a feeling that 'there is a certain duty by which I am bound to my guardian', the realization of the sacredness of that duty. And in this feeling there is a joy. If the child is inspired with this sense at that particular time, one will see that it will enjoy that feeling every time it experiences it.

When we look at life and see how many grown-up people have lost absolutely all regard for their guardians it makes one feel that the world is really wicked. There are so many souls who have no consideration for those who have brought them up from their childhood when they were helpless. It is very sad to see how many guardians and parents are treated neglectfully. And then in some rare case, when you see the devotion of a daughter to her aged mother, a daughter who has sacrificed everything in her life in order to make her aged mother comfortable and to help her, it seems so beautiful. And when you see a grown-up man who has a regard for his mother and father, so that while managing his affairs and having duties and responsibilities of life, he yet at the same time thinks of his aged parents, it is something so beautiful to see and there is such a blessing in it.

One can inspire this beautiful tendency in childhood; but if that time is missed then it becomes difficult. It is not only that it is beautiful to be able to give some pleasure and to render some service to the parents, but those who become considerate in their lives begin to see that this is the greatest privilege and blessing that one could have in life.

May a child give counsel to its parents? It would be disrespectful if even a grown-up child stood up and gave counsel to its parents, unless it was asked to do so. Besides a child is a child even if it is fifty years old, and if it does not feel a child with its parents it is missing a great deal in its life. There is a story of the King of Udaipur, who was still very sad a year after his mother's death. One day his friends told him, 'Now you have reached the age of fifty and you are a father, even a grandfather. Nobody's parents last for ever. As long as she lived it was a privilege, but now she is gone and you must forget your sorrow'. He said, 'Yes, I am trying to forget; but there is one thing I cannot forget, and that is the nickname by which she called me. Everyone is respectful towards me, everyone calls me "Maharana"; but she alone called me by a nickname, and I loved it so much.'

No matter what age one reaches, if one does not feel like a baby, like a child with one's parents, it is a pity. It is a great joy to feel like a baby, no matter at what age. It is a great privilege, a blessing in life when one's parents are living, and when one has that chance of acting like a baby. It is the most beautiful thing in the world.

No doubt it is very easy to be insolent, and it is very amusing to teach others; and when a person is grown-up he may also try to teach his parents. They are old and weak now, and perhaps also declining mentally; naturally they give in. But there is no beauty in it. The beauty is to give a counsel without giving counsel, if necessary even without speaking. On the other hand, thoughtful parents, when a child has won their confidence, naturally wish for counsel. But when the child has the right understanding he will have the right attitude, he will never make the counsel seem like a counsel; he will always put it in such a way that it will seem as if it came from the parents and not from himself.

The third ideal that one can inspire in the child is a sense of pride, a self-respecting attitude; because this is the time when the child could lose its self-respect and that little sense of pride or honour which is now growing in it. It is natural to see the child pleased with a toy or attracted to a sweet that is placed before it; but it is better still when you offer to the child a toy or a sweet which it likes and it refuses it out of self-respect. It is pleasant to see a child saying to its guardian, 'Please get me this,' and 'Buy this for me,' or 'I would like to have this'; but it is better still to see the child holding back its desire out of self-respect. If pride is not developed at that age, then what is life going to be without pride?

Nothing. In the days when communications were not as they are now, it happened that children of good families came to a country far from home and where they were unknown, either because they were exiled or because circumstances or destiny had brought them there. And what made them prove to be what they were was pride, not pearls or jewels or money or anything. A sense of honour is such a great treasure that, in the absence of all jewels and money and wealth, this will prove to be most valuable.

In what must this pride consist? It must consist in the sense of contentment. If the child understands, 'Where I am not wanted I need not be', or, 'No matter how much better an object belonging to another person may be, or how beautiful is the fruit or the flower, or anything that belongs to him, I must not even show that I would like to have it', that sense of honour is riches itself. How many parents strive all their life to collect money to give comfort to their children afterwards! But how much can they depend on that money, and especially at this time when money is changing so quickly in value that it takes no time for a rich man to become poor? If money makes a person rich, then those riches are not reliable. But the parents can give riches which cannot be taken away from the child; and these riches are in the form of ennobling its spirit.

May not the feeling of honour develop a false pride, one might ask, and how can one prevent this? This is the guardian's responsibility. Anything exaggerated and anything carried to the extreme is bad. One can become too proud and one can think too much of honour. But generally the life of the world is so wicked that instead of increasing the sense of honour it does the opposite. There are so many needs, there are so many wants; there are so many conditions and situations which instead of raising a person pull him down. Therefore the effort on the part of the guardian should be to give a hand to the soul to climb upward, instead of letting it go downward. There are many influences which pull downward. One must inspire the child with such pride and honour that in poverty or wealth, and in all conditions it may prove to be a noble soul.

Then there is a fourth ideal that one should inspire in the child, That ideal is thoughtfulness in speaking or in doing anything. This means the child must become conscious of its child's place; it must not try to take the place of the elder one. It is a child; it must keep its place. For instance, if two elderly people are discussing something and the child comes in and says, 'No, no, it is not so,' it is out of place. Maybe according to its mind it is not so, but it is not entitled to say so. It must keep its place. That is what is meant by thoughtfulness.

Care must be taken of everything; for instance, when the child wants to sit down somewhere, if it does not consider those who must be seated first, but first takes a place for itself, letting others wait; or if when entering a place or leaving it, the child goes forward and keeps back those who should go first; or when at the dinner-table, a child holds out his hand first, before the others have moved; all such things must be taken care of.

In speech, in movement, in action the child must be conscious of its childhood and must know its place. If not what happens? How few thoughtful people one meets in one's everyday life! When one sees the ordinary life in the world of today there is no end to the lack of consideration. Why? Because they have left out all those things which are of most importance in education; they have left them out in order to make room for mathematics. The primary cause of the loss of all the finer principles in the education given today is that it has left out the ideal.

And the fifth ideal that can be inspired in the child is the ideal of the unknown, of the unseen. If that ideal is not inspired, what does a person live for? Only to earn a loaf of bread? Only to strive in this life of competition day after day, ruining one's health, weakening one's mind, humbling one's spirit? And what does one gain? If earthly gain is all there is, it is a very small gain after all. If a higher ideal, a spiritual ideal, or God-ideal is not inspired in the child, then it is as you see today, thousands and millions of souls who are lost in the crowd, who do not know anything except living from day to day. Their whole energy is spent in the struggle to live, and there is a still greater struggle to live more comfortably; beyond this there seems nothing else. But how long can they be contented with this ideal? A time comes when they may lose their mind. They may have millions in the bank, and yet they are not satisfied because they cannot see where they are going and whether there is anything to look forward to. It is in childhood that the spirit is responsive, and if the God-ideal is inspired at that time then one has done what Christ has said, 'Seek ye first the kingdom of God . . . and all these things shall be added unto you'; one has given the child a start on the path of God; and that is the first lesson that should be given in childhood.

In training children the best way is not to show them that you are teaching them. The best thing is to be the friend of one's child. In a friendly talk with children one can inspire these things in them. Because as soon as a child knows that it is being taught it takes it heavily. But if you bring out the good that is in the child and the ideal that is in its spirit already, then the child will gladly listen to what you are saying. To rule the child is one thing, and to give loving and friendly counsel to a child is another thing. By ruling one cannot hammer these ideals into the head of a child, but by winning its affection and love you can very well train its spirit and tune it to the higher ideal.

The age of seven, eight, and nine years is considered childhood, early childhood. The beginning of this age is the beginning of a new life, a step forward into life. From seven, eight, and nine the child is conscious of the human sphere. Before that a child is conscious of the higher spheres, but at this time it is conscious of the human world. For the guardians this age of the child is of the greatest interest.

There was once a man in prison who offered the State all his wealth if he were allowed to come out of prison. It took a long time for the Government to decide. And when the Government decided that he should be released he said, 'No, now there is no purpose in coming out. There is a child at home, and this was the time of the greatest interest, to watch it grow, between seven and nine years old. Now that age is passed I prefer to finish my sentence'.

Early childhood is like soil that is just prepared for sowing the seed. It is such a great opportunity in the life of the child, and an even greater opportunity for the guardian to sow the seed of knowledge and of righteousness in the heart of the child.

There are three subjects of interest which may not be taught to the child, but the child may be helped to interest itself in them: drawing, music, and dancing. It is at this age that the movements of the child should become graceful. But once the guardian begins to teach the child, then it is a training. This is not the time to train the child, this is the time to give free expression to its soul; to let it dance in any way that it likes to dance, a natural dance; to draw pictures just as it wishes to draw them and paint just as it wishes to paint, without any direction given to it, only interest in its work. Also if the child wishes to play an instrument or sing, let it sing in whatever way it likes. Maybe a word here and there to help it, but not to correct it, not to give it lessons on these subjects, not to let it think it is being taught; the child should only feel that it is being helped.

When we study life keenly, we find that drawing, singing, and dancing are innate or inner inclinations. A child need not be taught, they come by themselves. Every normal child has a desire to sing, a desire to draw, and also a desire to dance. Only the child begins sometimes by drawing lines and figures on the wall and spoiling the wall. The guardians can check this inclination by giving the child pencil and paper and asking it to draw pictures on it. The child will feel proud to have the material to draw. Very often guardians become cross because a child has been drawing on the wall; but it cannot be helped, it is a natural inclination.

The next inclination is that of singing. Very often an energetic child will show this inclination by shouting, by making a noise, by raising its voice; and this can be controlled. It can be best controlled by showing appreciation for a little song that the child may sing. And if it does not know one, then let it learn one somewhere. A child who has the inclination to hear its own voice will be very glad to imitate any song it hears.

The third inclination, that of dancing, the child shows in jumping up and down and running from one corner to another. This shows restlessness and an inclination to move. And this activity can be controlled by showing appreciation for the dancing movements of little children.

There was a time when the ancient people thought very much about movements. And they were right in thinking thus about them; because whenever you see a person with awkward movements you will find something awkward in his character. A person who is deficient in brain will always show it in the awkwardness of his movements. If movements have so much to do with a person's evolution, with his mentality, then graceful movements will always help the mentality of a person. The child which is naturally inclined to movement, will take interest if it is directed towards moving with rhythm.

One might think it difficult to teach a child dancing, but one need not teach it dancing. One has only to teach the child action; for instance to turn, to take something from the ground or from the mantelpiece, to move something, any such everyday actions, and naturally all these actions turn into a dance. Besides children are very imitative, and anything that appeals to them they readily imitate. If they see graceful movements they are most eager to imitate them. That is the age when the imitating faculty begins to develop. Is it then good for children of that age to take them to dancing performances and exhibitions of pictures? Sometimes it is good, as long as one knows where one is taking them and what kind of performance it is.

There are three things that a child may be taught at this particular time: perseverance, patience, and endurance. The child may be taught perseverance in anything that it is engaged in doing. Perhaps it is mending a toy, or doing some other work; one should help the child, encourage it to continue and not to leave it before it is finished. For however small this may appear, when this habit is formed, it will show later on in big things. A soul who has learned perseverance in childhood will show a tendency all his life to finish everything that he undertakes.

Frequently we see that this tendency is lacking among grown-up people; and this is very often the cause of their failure in life. And if their mind is restless, then it is still worse. They take up something today, and then after a week their interest is gone and there is something else; and they accomplish nothing in their lives. Life is a great opportunity, and the one who does not complete the thing he has undertaken, however small, certainly loses most in life.

Accomplishment is more valuable than what is accomplished. For instance, if a person has loosened a knot in a string, apparently he has not gained anything, the time has been spent on a very small thing; and yet the action of completing it is useful, he has built something in his spirit that will be useful to him when he wants to accomplish great works.

And now coming to the subject of patience, how can a child be taught patience? By teaching it to wait. Because a child is very impatient by nature, and if this tendency remains, then after that child is grown-up it will give it great unhappiness. When a person has no patience life becomes death for him. Patience is like death, but not to have patience is worse than death. Besides patience produces wonderful fruits, and patience is a quality which is beyond comparison with any other qualities in the world. If there is anything that gives kingliness to the soul, it is patience. What was the secret of the masters who have accomplished great things, who have inspired many and who have helped many souls? Their secret was patience. This is the time to sow the seed of patience in the child. In little things you can give the child the habit of patience. In asking for food, in wanting to go out to play, and in many other things a child shows lack of patience; yet if at that time, without hurting it, one gives it the habit of patience, the child will begin to show nobleness of spirit.

The third thing is endurance. One might ask, 'We have so much to endure in life when we are grown-up, why must we make a child endure at that age?' But the answer is that for the very reason that life will make it endure when it is grown-up, let it know from this time that there is such a thing as endurance and that every soul has to go through this. No doubt it is painful for the loving guardian to see the child develop the faculty of endurance, but at the same time it would be more painful if the child were to grow up without this faculty. And in what way can one teach the child this? From morning till evening in the life of a child there are a thousand things happening; so many times it falls, and so many times it hurts itself, and so many times it has to swallow a bitter pill; and every time that it is not inclined to go through something that is good for it to go through, one should give it courage and strength and a word of encouragement or of advice, appreciating its endurance. In this way it will develop the enduring faculty.

In teaching the child, the best method is not to let it know that

you are teaching. Teach it without the child knowing it. And that can be done by showing appreciation for the least little thing it does which you wish to develop in its spirit. The ego is born with pride, even in the child; and if you appreciate something, the child likes it too, and even sometimes more than the grown-up, because grown-up people have lost faith in words.

Very often people teach wrong nursery rhymes. It is not only a waste of time, but it has a bad effect on the child. Sometimes they are useless words, and sometimes they are meaningless words, and sometimes they are words of suggestion which may just as well be kept away from the mind of the child. Every rhyme that only rhymes is not beneficial; it must have some sense in it. And therefore the guardian must know first what he is teaching before teaching the child.

It is the same with stories. The best method of teaching children is to teach them with stories. There are fables that interest children very much, and also there is a meaning to understand. If the guardians will explain to them the meaning that is in that fable the children will become still more interested in it, and at the same time they will learn something. A story need not be always very instructive; even grown-up people do not like that. The most interesting story for children is a funny story; and if one can put some little meaning into a comical story, that is the best thing one can do. They remember it, and at the same time the sense remains concealed in the story; and as they grow the sense begins to emerge, and one day they understand what it means.

There is a fable of a donkey and a camel. Once a donkey went to a camel and said, 'Camel Uncle, I would like very much to go grazing with you.' The camel said, 'Yes, I will come with you tomorrow.' And so they went into a field. It took a long time for the camel to feed himself, but the donkey fed himself very quickly. After the donkey had finished his dinner he said, 'Camel Uncle, I am so happy, first to have your friendship and then to be here in the field. I feel like singing and I would very much like you to dance.' The camel said, 'I have not yet finished my meal but you seem to be ready.' 'Well', said the donkey, 'if you are not ready I will try my voice'. And the donkey began to try his voice. And the farmer came with a stick in his hand, but the donkey jumped out of the way and the camel was beaten.

When next day the donkey went to invite Uncle Camel, the camel said, 'I· am too ill; your way is different and my way is different. From today we will part.'

This story shows the sense of friendship between the one who is dignified and the one who has no sense of dignity.

If a young child asks a question about his origin, the answer one must give is: God. This question gives one an opening to sow the seed of the God-ideal in the heart of the child.

It is always good to tell children stories from the Bible or other sacred scriptures, but the person who puts them in a form that the child can understand must be very wise. If not, as the stories are, sometimes they are not proper stories to teach children; also the time of the Old Testament was a different time, and there are some stories which do not suit the present time. It is always a good thing for the guardian to make his own stories; to get the ideas out of different books and to put them into his own story and then give them to the children. Once a wise guardian was asked by a child, 'But is it a real story?' and he said, 'As a story it is real'.

It is learning while playing, for no one is so interested in stories as little children; and if one makes use of that interest for their benefit, one has the greatest opportunity to put wonderful ideas into their minds with the stories. In no other way will the child absorb ideals as it will do in the form of stories. The stories told in its early childhood will remain with it all through its life. It will never forget them. Maybe that every year, as the child grows, that story will have another meaning; and so there will be a

continual development of the ideal, which will become a great blessing in the life of the child.

The time between the ages of ten and twelve years may be called middle childhood. It is in this period that a child begins to be distinguished as a girl-child or a boy-child; and each must be given its particular direction, for a girl a girl's direction and for a boy a boy's direction. At home an education can be given which is not to be expected at school. Even if the same subjects were taught at school it would not be the same as what a child learns at home. Therefore even when the child is going to school there still remains a responsibility for the guardians to give it home education apart from its studies in the school.

For the intellectual development of the child it is of great importance that it becomes familiar with nature. It must not be done as a lesson; it must be done as a friendly talk to explain to the child about plants, trees, insects, birds, animals. And when it is given by the spoken word the effect is quite different from the reading of natural science or any other studies of nature that the child may make. It wakens its interest and it develops its knowledge, it deepens in it a feeling for nature; and it will later culminate in the wakening of the faculty of communicating with nature, which is the principal thing for every soul in his spiritual development.

A soul who is not close to nature is far away from what is called spirituality. In order to be spiritual one must communicate, and especially one must communicate with nature; one must feel nature. There is so much to be learned from plant life, from birds, animals, insects, that once a child begins to take an interest in that subject, everything becomes a symbolical expression of the inner truth. If the child is deeply interested in the knowledge of nature, that shows that it has taken the first step on the path of philosophical truth.

The next thing is to acquaint the child with the customs of the country where it was born and has to live. It is the absence of this knowledge that makes people continue their old customs without knowing what they are and why they are; people go on sometimes for thousands of years following the same custom and yet not knowing the meaning of it. People in the East are very keen on their ancient customs, and very often they have followed those customs for more than a thousand years without knowing why and what is in them; they do it only because it is a custom. But it happens also in the West, where in some places there is a festival almost every day. It would be good for a child to know why such a custom exists, what is the good of it, what is the meaning of it, what we derive from it and what it suggests. It is interesting to celebrate a fête and to be gay and joyous; but one can make merry every day and yet achieve nothing. Besides life is an opportunity and every day and every hour of life is of the greatest importance; and if one allows so much of one's time to be given to customs of the country there is no end to it.

Every generation must take a step forward in evolution, and it can do it better by understanding life better. The guardians can help the child very much by making it understand life. And the best way of educating the child is not to give one's opinion about these customs, not to say directly that this is a good or a bad custom; only to explain the psychology of it and the meaning of the custom, and let the child see for itself if it is a custom worth following or better forgotten.

The third thing one can help the child to understand is something about the people of its country; what they were and what they are, their characteristics, their inclinations and their aspirations; and let the child imagine what it would like its world to be. This also gives it an opportunity of reconstruction as the world evolves.

And the fourth thing is to acquaint the child with its own family. Very often it happens that a child knows about China and

Japan, and about Egypt and Persia, having read about them, and it does not know the name of its grandfather. If it knows something about its family, its genealogy, it will be able to control life better. Maybe there are things that the child will follow, that it will adopt for its betterment; and it may be that there are things that it will correct in itself; maybe it wishes to repair some harm that was done before. In both cases the child will be able to manage its life better as it goes on.

If a soul is not interested in knowing about its own family, when it is grown-up it will not be interested in knowing about the source from whence it comes. Because this is the first point from which it can go further, until it reaches to that source, to that family, from whence it truly comes; and so in reality this is leading the child to God. For instance, a child is interested in knowing about its father, its mother, its grandfather, its grandmother, and perhaps about its great-grandfather; but where does it lead to? It only leads from the world of illusion to the source of reality. It gives the child an excuse to enquire further into life, and where it has come from; and in the end it will come to the conception of the source, which is the Source of all. And in this way it will find one day that the whole of humanity is a family, and that in the end we all meet in the same place where we have come from. When the child is grown-up it will change its whole attitude towards human beings; the narrowness will vanish, and a broad outlook will come to him of itself.

As the fifth aspect of knowledge one should give the child a little introduction to metaphysics, not much, just enough for it to know that there is a soul, that there is a mind, that there is a body; that there is a relation between the soul and the mind, and the mind and the body. For instance, if a child asks, 'What is the soul?' the shortest answer will be, 'Your innermost being, your invisible self, your self which is covered by your body. But that self is your real self, the body is only a covering.' Very often one little idea about a metaphysical truth goes into the heart of a child like a spark of fire which slowly blazes into a flame, a flame which will guide it through its whole life.

This is the period in the life of a child when the guardian must find out the trend of its mind, and which way it will take in life. This does not mean which profession it will take or what work it will do, only one should know if the child has a literary, a mechanical, an idealistic, or a religious trend of mind. And once the guardian has understood this it is better to give the child a suitable impression. For instance, when the guardian has found out that the child has a literary trend of mind, and there is a great man lecturing in the city, it is good to take the child there. If it does not understand one word it does not matter. Let it be there, let it look at what is going on, and that impression will remain with the child for its whole life; and maybe that impression will help the child to become like the one it has seen.

At the age of ten, eleven, and twelve the child is most imitative, and if you know the bent of its mind, and if you give it an impression which it may imitate and which would be good for it to imitate, this means that you are setting it on the road which will lead to its destination. The best thing one can do in the life of a child is to give it good impressions, to show it wonderful personalities and wonderful works. Nothing in the world can help a child more than a good impression.

One might ask if one should develop only what is the child's special trend of mind. Should one not also show him another direction? Yes, but gently. And then one must see if the child has a tendency, an inclination, towards it. For instance, if a child shows more tendency to become a mechanician and if you urge it to become a violinist, in the end this will prove to be disastrous. The child will be neither a mechanician nor a violinist. It is better to watch the bent of the child's mind.

Regarding the cultivation of different qualities in the child,

this can best be done with each child by teaching it to sing and play, and by giving it ear-training and rhythmic movements. If a child is inclined to sing it is best for it to sing; but if the child is not inclined to sing, but wants to play an instrument, it is best to give it an instrument to play. Which instrument is the best? This one cannot say. But an easy instrument should be given first; and afterwards, if the child wants another instrument which he likes better, then one should give it that instrument.

In the case of a girl it is better that she learns rhythmic movements; in the case of a boy it is better that he learns gymnastics. For a girl rhythmic movements serve the same purpose, and yet they do not hurt her girlish characteristics. For the boy gymnastics suffice, and these keep each in their own direction. The energy in a boy that makes him so restless and uncomfortable will be used in gymnastics, and that will bring about balance of mind.

Should every child be taught music? Yes; in the first place there is no child who is not inclined towards music; it is the grown-up who becomes disinclined towards music. There is an Arabian story that when God commanded the soul to enter the body of clay He had made, the first body of man, the soul refused to enter it. The soul said, 'I am free to move about in any sphere I like, and I have the limitless strength and power I derive from Thee; I do not want to enter into this body of clay. To me it looks like a prison.' Then God asked the angels to play on their harps; and the soul on hearing this music began to dance and went into ecstasy. It entered the body unknowingly and was caught in this prison.

Therefore no soul comes on earth without a feeling for music. It is only when souls have become dense after having come to the earth that they lose that feeling. But when someone has lost interest in music one should know that that person is not living; there is something that was living in that person that is now dead.

It is not necessary for every child to be brought up to be a musician, but elementary teaching of music is necessary for every child. It will help it in every walk of life. Whatever it may do a musical training will help it. And therefore musical training must not be considered as a branch or as one part of education but as the foundation for the child's whole life.

The time between the ages of ten and twelve years is the period that finishes a cycle, the first cycle in the life of every soul. Mystics consider each cycle as twelve years. Therefore these last three years of the first cycle are of very great importance in the life of the child. During this particular period at the ages of ten, eleven, and twelve, what is taught is like the finishing touch given by an artist after having painted a picture; and after this another cycle begins.

The time of preparing children for the next cycle is a most important period. If the child by this time has not been taught, has not been corrected, has not been given that direction which it ought to have taken, then later on it will be difficult; for the most important period has passed. The more guardians understand of their responsibility, the more they will realize that if things were not taught which should have been taught at that time they can never be taught later.

The appropriate direction must be given to the girls and to the boys. One cannot drive both with the same whip. For instance, a word of displeasure will touch the boy on the surface and the girl to the depth; and it is the same with a word of appreciation. Often with the boy it will go in at one ear and out at the other, whereas the girl will keep it with her perhaps for her whole life. Those who think that boys and girls can both be directed in the same way will find in the end that they made a great mistake. The psychology of the boy is quite different from the girl's, and for each a special method must be used in order to bring them up.

If the girl or the boy receives a word of admiration or of blame,

it must be given in different terms and in different words; and one should be most lenient towards the girl, whereas it does not matter so much with the boy. Often the boy takes a punishment and after half an hour, or even before half an hour has passed, he forgets it; and often a girl remembers it for months and months; it affects her most deeply. Besides there are certain characteristics to be developed in the boy and certain characteristics to be developed in the girl; and you cannot call them virtues for both. For instance, courage in the boy, modesty in the girl; common sense in the boy, idealism in the girl; responsibility in the boy, duty in the girl; God-ideal in the boy, religion in the girl; also thought in the boy, consideration in the girl.

One may ask why it is necessary to develop the inherent qualities of boys and girls; why not pay attention first to their opposites? The reason is this, that any quality that is an inherent quality is born in a person because that quality will lead to the purpose of his life. For instance the lion is given the quality of the lion; that is the purpose, that is his destiny; and the deer is given the quality needed for the purpose of his life. But if the lion had the deer quality or the deer had the lion quality, neither would be properly equipped for living in the world. What the deer is shows in its own quality, what the lion is shows in its own quality. One must not think it is not necessary for the other quality to come to the boy or girl; but what should be developed is the particular quality, and the other quality will come by itself. It does not mean that a boy must not have those qualities which have been said to belong to a girl. For instance, if the boy is without any ideal he is useless; but the ideal will come; in the girl, however, it must be planted, it must be developed.

It is the psychology of the boy and the girl which makes it necessary to give certain things to the boy and certain things to the girl; but as they develop they take each other's qualities; with development it comes naturally. Balance is best, whether in the boy or in the girl; and balance comes through opposite qualities. The work of the teacher is not to teach balance, the work of the teacher is to teach qualities; life will bring about balance by itself, as long as boys and girls are taught that particular quality which belongs to them.

The question arises how children should answer the different demands of life, such as helping at home, helping outside, seeing friends, seeing strangers. Children of ten, eleven, and twelve need not be given particular work to do at home, but at the same time they should be made acquainted with the duties of the household and with the work in outside life, so that as they grow up they may understand and appreciate the responsibility and the duties of their guardians.

With friends of the family children should have a respectful attitude, the same attitude they have towards their own guardians or parents. One day the Prophet heard his children calling a servant by his name, and the Prophet said, 'No, children, he is older than you. Call him uncle.' This ideal was taught from the beginning, in order that as they grew up they might attract more friends, instead of offending friends of the house. Also it shows a beautiful manner in the child to have a friendly outlook and a respectful attitude towards the friends of the family. And when children of that age meet strangers, the strangers can understand from the manner of the children what home, what family they belong to, what education, what training they have been given. If they are rude, thoughtless, inconsiderate, or ill-mannered, they represent their family in this way. Therefore it is the responsibility and the duty of the guardian to make the children aware of these rules of everyday life.

The period between ten and twelve is the period when children must be taught to practise whatever work is given to them, whether it be music, painting, drawing, or anything else. This is the time when they must learn to concentrate upon that work, stick to that work, and not let their minds be disturbed by anything outside; because later on this faculty will prove to be the foundation of spiritual development.

And then comes a still more delicate question, and that is that in their food, in their fancies, in their clothes, they must not have too much their own way; because this is not the time when they should be thinking very much about clothes or about the food they eat or about anything like that; it is the time when they should be quite unaware of it. Whatever is given to them they should take gratefully, thankfully; the days of fancy and fantasy will come afterwards. And if care is not taken of that side of children's nature, it will develop disagreeably and later on it will take the form of a very undesirable spirit.

How can this be done? It should be done, not by correcting them nor by impressing rules upon them, but by making them see the pleasure of contentment; and the thought must be impressed upon them that this is the time when they must put their mind to work. By gentle counsel and friendly advice they will soon understand. A guardian once told a little girl who was very fond of looking in the mirror, 'Jinns can peep through the mirror, and you must look out for them; people who look in the mirror too many times will have to meet jinns'. And from that time that little child showed less and less of that tendency. One may ask if there is any harm in looking in the mirror. There is; looking in the mirror makes one self-conscious, and self-consciousness makes one nervous. And all the tragedy of life comes from self-consciousness when it culminates in self-pity.

It is a very delicate work to train the child without its realizing that it is being taught. Everything one teaches it must be in such a way that the child does not know that a certain rule or principle is imposed upon it; that is the way to work with it. In laughter, in smiles, in stories, in friendly conversation, things can be told to children that they will always remember; but as soon as they are corrected and one imposes a certain principle upon them they begin to feel the burden of it.

It must be remembered that life is an opportunity, and this particular period of ten, eleven, and twelve years is a most wonderful opportunity. This is the period when children drink in and assimilate any knowledge, and that knowledge grows with them in their growth. Very often the knowledge of the various rules of life can be given to them in a very mild form by telling stories, because a story gives a wonderful picture of life and yet they do not feel the burden of the teaching. They are interested; and very often after the story children will even ask, 'What does it mean, what do we get from it?' And when that happens then one should know that one has the greatest opportunity of tuning the child's spirit to the knowledge and the consciousness to which one wishes to tune it.

4
The Education of Youth

THE age between thirteen, fourteen, and fifteen years is the time when childhood is ending, and it is the beginning of youth. On one side there is the urge of youth and on the other side childhood ending; it brings about an inner struggle in the child. The child is neither a youth nor a child, and therefore there is a struggle in its being. That is why some children appear to be very nervous at that time. This age is the period of Kemal, the period of inner conflict. And when the guardian is unaware of this inner conflict, he will find in the child a very troublesome element showing itself in many forms; but when the guardian understands that this time in the life of the child is a time of conflict, he will treat it differently. It is the time when the child must be handled most carefully. A child will show moments of passiveness and moments of activeness; at times the child will show presence of mind and at other times it will be absent-minded. The mind of the child is beginning to form at that time, and the foundation of the mind is being laid in that period.

In the period of Kemal three aspects of knowledge should be taught to the child: the knowledge of the land, of the water, and of the sky. The knowledge of the land is the knowledge of what is produced in the land, in the mineral and vegetable kingdoms. The knowledge of the water is of the creatures that live in the water, the dangers of the water, and the way that men travel and have travelled over the sea. The knowledge of the sky is about the stars and planets, the sun and the moon and the effect of wind and storm. The reason why this particular knowledge should be given at this time is that the mind is not yet definitely formed, and it should be based from the beginning on wide lines, in order that a wide building may be created on that foundation.

At that time, it is better to help the child, whether boy or girl, to keep a passive rather than an active attitude, because it is the time of absorption and not the time of expression. By urging a passive attitude upon the child one will only make it uncomfortable; but by cultivating that attitude gently, without allowing the child to know it, one will prepare the soil of its mind for a better purpose. It is, however, a difficult problem. One can cultivate a passive attitude in the child by trying to attract its interest to one's words and one's actions.

It is not desirable to force the development of spiritual tendencies in early youth; but it is desirable to help to develop what little spiritual tendency there is.

Youth is the time for definite religious education. If that time is past, then a person is always shy of taking part in religion. However much attracted he may be to religion and to the religious ideal, he feels awkward and shy about it, and he does not come forward to take his part in it. One may ask if it is better to bring a child up first in one religion and to make it acquainted with other religions later on, or to teach it from the beginning that all religions are one. First the child must know one religion in order to know all religions. If it has not come to understand one religion it will not come to the understanding of all religions. Broadness is the result and not the beginning. If you make a person too broad in the beginning, in the end he will become narrow.

The culture of the mind has five different aspects. First, thought and imagination. Thought is one thing, and imagination is another. Very often people confuse these two words. Thinking is an automatic action of mind, there is no will-power behind it. Therefore the dream is an imagination; only it is called a dream because it is more concrete; when a person is asleep and the senses are closed there is nothing but the imagination before the mind. But in the case of imagination in the waking state there is on one side imagination and on the other side the action of the five senses, and then imagination plays a passive part.

In helping the child to cultivate thought and imagination one may also make a mistake. Once I visited a school of thought-culture. They had made a new system, and I went to see it. There were ten or twelve children standing, and the teacher said, 'Look, what is there here?' There was nothing but a plain board before them. One child says, 'A lily.' The teacher says 'All right.' To another child he says, 'Look, what is here?' The other child looks and says, 'A red rose.' The teacher is satisfied. And to the third child he says, 'See, what is here?' The child says, 'It is a pink rose', and again the teacher is satisfied. And then he asks another child to tell what is there, and the child says, 'I do not see anything'. I thought to myself, 'He is the one who has some sense, for he did not tell a lie.'

Now, what good will it do to the children, who say whatever comes into their heads, but have seen nothing? It is only making them imaginative and after that, what? Only worse; and after that still worse. The fate of these ten or twelve children will be the worst fate. Imagine them learning for five or six years this kind of thought-culture, by which they allow their imagination to run freely and believe that they see what they have imagined with their eyes on the board! It can only lead to what might be called mediumistic culture.

The right way of helping the imagination of the child is to direct its attention to all that is beautiful, and then see what it would like to add to it to complete the beauty, be it the beauty of line, of colour, of notes, or of rhythm, be it the beauty of idea, beauty of action, or beauty of meaning. In this way the child's imagination could develop. If one asks the child, 'What would you do in this situation?' 'What would you like to do to make it complete?' 'What would you do to make it more beautiful?', in this way one helps the child to develop its faculty of imagination.

But then comes the question of how to develop a child's thought. The thought of a child cannot be developed by getting it to think on love, or on kindness, or goodness, or anything like that. As soon as the child is given a thought to hold on to it feels uncomfortable, uneasy, just as a mule would feel the burden on its back. The best way is to find out what it is thinking of and to strengthen that thought, if the thought is desirable.

For example, a child said to its guardian, 'I would like to have a magic wand. Where could I get it?' The guardian said, 'If you had a magic wand what would you do with it?' The child answered, 'I heard that if a person has a magic wand, he has only to wave it and everything will come.' So the guardian said, 'What do you wish?' At first the child hesitated, because he felt very shy about telling his wish, but in the end he expressed his wish. As soon as the guardian knew he said, 'You do not need a magic wand; the wish itself is a power if you can think about it.' The child said, 'I always think about it.' The guardian said, 'Think about it still more.' It is not giving a child a new thought, but just strengthening its thought. From that moment the child who was looking for a magic wand thought the magic wand was in itself; that if it thought about the magic wand it would get what it wanted.

A child always has a good memory, but it acts only in things it is interested in. Where the child has no interest it will not remember. It does not mean that it cannot remember, but that it will not remember. It is not a mistake of the child's memory, but it is the mistake of those who force upon its memory something that will not stay there. And very often the greatest mistake of school-teachers is that they force upon the mind of the child something in which it is not interested, that it does not want to look at, or think about. How cruel it is that in order that the child should pass an examination, its mind should be forced and urged to hold an idea which it is not capable of holding! The best way of developing a child's memory is to give it something it remembers, likes, and is interested in, and to ask the child about it, to take an interest in it oneself and to keep that flame burning.

Many children do not like the study of mathematics. If it is not their temperament, if it is not in their nature they will not like it. Mathematics are easy for those who have that temperament, who are born with that tendency; but there is another tendency which is quite opposite to figures, to mathematics.

When a child is interested, for instance, in poetry, and yet cannot remember it, this shows that it has no concentration; but that will improve by giving the child a greater interest in poetry, and encouraging it to read it more and to recite it, and by showing appreciation of what it does. Very often a guardian is interested in telling a story to a child, but is not interested in hearing that story from the child. But this is a great training if one can do it; if having told a story to the child one asks it to tell the story again after three months, and then sees how its memory works. In this way memory can be developed.

Some children have the reasoning faculty developed in them and others have not. But this is a faculty upon which the future of the child depends, upon which its whole life depends. Where the reasoning faculty is not developed there is always a danger for its life. It can be easily cultivated in the child by asking questions for and against everything: if it must be, why it must be; and if it must not be, why it must not be; and sometimes quite the contrary question. When a child says, 'This is right', it must be asked why it is right; if the child says, 'This is wrong', it must be asked why it is wrong. The guardian must take the same attitude that the child has, always asking why, instead of letting the child ask why. The guardian must become a child and ask why of everything; and in this way reasoning is developed. Any child that shows the quality of reasoning has the promise of a wonderful future before it.

It is not always advisable to play with children's emotions. Often it might be a pleasure to the guardian to see how the child is affected by a certain thought, by a certain word. But by doing this one weakens that faculty. The best thing is to keep the feeling of the child untouched, in order that this deepest faculty may grow still deeper and stronger, so that when the child comes to the age when its emotion must show itself, it is perfected.

In the culture of mind the most important problem is the thought of 'I'; and this thought develops very strongly in a child of thirteen, fourteen, and fifteen. It is very keen about saying I and my. And if this faculty is softened at that particular period in childhood, while the child is growing up, it will be much better. This faculty shows itself especially when the child is cross, when it is in a temper, when it wants to defend itself, and when it wants to express, 'This I own, this is mine, and nobody else must touch it, and nobody else must take it.' At such times it must be softened. At thirteen, fourteen, and fifteen the child is more thoughtful, and if at times of anger there is an effort made by the guardians to help it to look at things rightly and from their point of view, it is easier at this time than it was in its early childhood.

Youth is divided into three parts. Thirteen, fourteen, and fifteen years are early youth; sixteen, seventeen, and eighteen, the middle part of youth; nineteen, twenty and twenty-one, complete youth.

There is a tendency on the part of guardians to encourage the development of a youth in whatever direction he chooses to take. But to encourage a youth in any direction is like urging on a very energetic horse which is already running fast. What a youth needs most is not encouragement; what he needs most is balance. The tendency of a youth, both in the right direction and the wrong direction, may prove unsatisfactory in the end if his action is not evenly balanced.

There are two important things to be considered by guardians in the development of the youth. One is that very often guardians think this is the same child who used to be a baby and a little child running about, and they go on treating the youth in the same way as they have done before. They underestimate his comprehension, his maturity of mind, the development of his spirit; and in this way very often they delude themselves. And then there are others who take the opposite course. When the youth begins to say things that show a greater intelligence, they believe that they can tell him anything and everything, without waiting for the appropriate time to mention a certain thing, a certain idea. And therefore mistakes may be made both by considering a youth to be an experienced person, and also by considering him to be still a child that does not know anything.

It is mostly the education of the home, if it is not given properly, that spoils a youth. The time of youth is a time of nervousness, of restlessness, and of agitation. If the education given at home antagonizes the youth, he is spoiled for ever. If the good opinion that he had before of his guardians is changed, then youth is the time when guardian and child become estranged; youth builds a wall between the guardian and the growing child. The growing child finds consolation with friends, with neighbours, with acquaintances, who sometimes take advantage by saying, 'Yes, you are right. Your people at home do not understand you. It is a great pity, it is a shame'; and that great opportunity of making the link with the youth more strong is lost by the guardians who do not understand this situation properly. A child who shows friendship, response, and the feeling of comradeship with the guardian during his youth, will be a great friend all his life.

It is like training a horse. There is a certain time when a horse learns to obey, but if at that time the trainer makes a mistake, that mistake remains for ever in the horse. And if at the time of maturity of its mind, when the horse is beginning to respond to the trainer, it is given a right direction, then all through life that horse works rightly.

Some guardians show their helplessness in not being able to control a youth, and criticize the youth who is not under their control and does not listen to them; they think it is hopeless, that the youth is spoiled, and that he is gone out of their hands. They help the child very little, because they are only conscious of his bad points; and by showing their dissatisfaction they do not help the youth, they spoil him. The guardians need not be severe with the youth, they need not be too firm, nor too pessimistic in regard to his advancement. The more they trust him and the more they have confidence in themselves, the more they are able to help the child. Nothing helps more than trusting in the good points of the youth, appreciating them, and encouraging him in that direction.

There are, however, others who out of their love and sympathy spoil the youth. They pour out so much love and sympathy that it blinds them in what they are doing. Also the child is not meant to be for ever with the guardians. What will happen when the guardian is not there and the child has to face the world? Everybody will not spoil him, everybody will not give sympathy; and then the life of the child in the world will become wretched. Often children who happen to be the only child of their parents or in the family, and who are much cared for and receive much sympathy and love, become so spoiled that the very sympathy and love that has been given them proves to be a bitter pill. They never receive it again in life, and all through life they suffer for it.

It is wiser for the guardians to make a point of decreasing the

strong hold that they had on a child as it grows to become a youth. But how can they decrease it? Just as a rider makes the rein looser and looser, but gradually. Those who do not understand this have kept it firm in childhood, and then in youth have let it go. But it must be loosened gradually, and it must be loosened on the lines of the child's development. At every step forward in development of personality, of humanity, one must trust the youth and give that much more freedom of thought and action, yet holding the rein and keeping it firm, being conscious of the responsibility of the guardians to help the youth through that most critical period.

The best way of helping the youth is to give him desirable impressions of conditions, of situations, of personalities, and in this way, by giving him impressions, to let the child learn by himself without being taught in words.

There is a story of a father who saw that his young son had a tendency to certain vices. He told him often to keep away from them but the boy would not listen. He did everything in his power; in the end, when he was dying, he called his son and said, 'Now I will never tell you any more not to do things that you have always liked to do. But will you remember the last words of your father, that whenever you want to gamble you must gamble with the greatest gamblers, and whenever you feel like drinking you must drink with great drunkards.' The son thought these last words more desirable than anything he had heard from his father before. And when he went to gamble he began to ask people, 'Who are the great gamblers in the city?' They said, 'Great gamblers are not to be found in gambling houses. You must go and look for them outside the city.' So when he had heard their names he went there. He found that they were playing with pebbles, because they had lost all the money they had. And he said, 'I have heard a great deal about you people, and here you are playing with pebbles. I thought you would be playing for millions of pounds!' They said, 'No, we played for millions, and now we are playing for pebbles. Come along, if you wish to play with us. We have nothing more left.'

He got a lesson from this and he said, 'Nothing doing in this direction. Now I must go somewhere else to find great drunkards.' And the people in the city gave him two or three names of well-known drunkards and he went there. He did not find any bottles, any drink, nor anything. And he said to them, 'I have heard your names. Everybody talks about you; you are great drunkards. But there are no bottles; what are you drinking?' They said, 'All the money we had was spent in drinking. No money is left. We have now some snakes. When we want to drink we let the snakes bite us; that gives us a kind of intoxication. If you like we will bring a snake for you.' And he ran away and never came near them again. That gave him another lesson.

The education of youth depends mostly upon impressions. Sometimes you may make a youth read books and that will not help; and sometimes you may tell the youth fifty times or a hundred times, 'This is right', 'This is not right', 'This is not good', and he will never listen. But once you show him the phenomena, the example of what you are saying, and let the youth see with his own eyes what are the effects of different causes, then the teaching is given in an objective way; and in this manner wise guardians educate a youth.

5
The Education of Children

ON THE education of children depends the future of nations. To consider the education of children is to prepare for future generations. The heart of the child is like a photographic plate without any impressions on it, ready to reflect all that it is exposed to. All the good qualities which help to fulfil the purpose of life are the natural inheritance that every soul brings to the earth; and almost all the bad traits that mankind shows in its nature are as a rule acquired after birth. This shows that goodness is natural and badness unnatural. Therefore the child who has not yet had the opportunity of acquiring bad traits in life can, if helped, develop the natural goodness that is in its soul.

Education is not necessarily a qualification for making one's life successful, nor for safeguarding one's own interests; it is really a qualification for a fuller life, a life of thought for oneself and of consideration for others. Education is that which gradually expands in its length and breadth, horizontally and perpendicularly. We may further explain this as being the knowledge of oneself and of one's surroundings; the knowledge of others, both those who are known to us and those who are unknown and away; the knowledge of the conditions of human nature and of life's demands; and the knowledge of cause and effect, which leads in the end to the knowledge of the world within and without.

No doubt it is difficult to think of vast knowledge of life in connection with a child, but we must remember that as a rule the grown-ups underestimate the capacity of a child's mind, which is very often more eager to understand and more capable of comprehension than that of a grown-up person. Although you cannot start with a deep subject at the beginning of a child's education, you can always keep before you the large design you have in view and wish to reach.

The reason why the earliest remembrances of childhood have such a peculiarly vivid significance, is that we repeat after coming to the earth the same process through which the soul has passed. As the child grows it loses its innocence, so that it seems removed from the world of the angels. Infancy is still expressive of the angelic sphere; childhood expresses the sphere of the jinns; youth is the expression of the human world. And when one goes on one comes closer again to the higher spheres.

The child is more open to perceive, as its mind is free from worries and the excitement of life. The child is more willing to believe, for its mind is free from any pre-conceived idea. The child can look at things rightly, because its mind is not yet fixed on strong likes and dislikes. The child has already an inclination towards friendship, for animosity is unknown to it; and therefore the moral which should be the central theme of education, and which from beginning to end teaches the lesson of friendship, has full scope in the heart of a child.

The great fault of modern education has been that, with all its advanced methods of training children, it has missed what is most important: namely the lesson of unselfishness. Man thinks that an unselfish person is incapable of guarding his own interests in life; but however much it may appear so it is not so in reality. A selfish person is a disappointment to others, and in the end a disadvantage to himself. Mankind is interdependent, and the happiness of each depends upon the happiness of all, and it is this lesson that humanity has to learn today as the first and the last lesson.

Music is the basis of the whole of creation. In reality the whole of creation is music, and what we call music is simply a miniature of the original music, which is creation itself, expressed in tone and rhythm. The Hindus call tone, or sound, *Nada Brahma*, which means Sound-Creator. No scientist can deny the truth that the entire creation is movement. The nature of movement is expressed in tone and rhythm. There is no movement which is not also a sound, although it may not be audible to the human ear, and there is no movement without rhythm; for there cannot be a movement unless it marks two, just as no straight line can be without two ends. With every movement one counts its first activity as one and the next as two. As the conductor's baton marks time for the orchestra: one-two, one-two, so one can mark the movement of every activity.

The whole of nature, in the change of seasons and of night and day, expresses rhythm; and the entire cosmic system shows in its working the law of rhythm. The ever-moving sea and the tides are examples of nature's rhythm. The entire universe being created on these two principles, the greatest appeal that can be made to a living creature is by means of tone and rhythm. The whole mechanism of man's body and the pulsation of his heart, all follow rhythm; this proves that every activity of life is an expression of tone and rhythm. Tone and rhythm constitute music; therefore music should be the principal means of perfecting the education of a child.

The infant begins its first activity in life by making a noise, trying to speak or moving its hands and legs to a certain rhythm. If the same faculty which every infant shows naturally is taken as the basis of his education, one can educate even an infant. The education given at the earliest age is invaluable to the child, for as the child grows, it acquires certain habits by itself; and once it has become fixed in its way of looking at things and thinking and behaving, these habits are hard to change. It is just like letting the rainwater make its own way instead of digging a canal to take the water to the farm or garden. In this way a child's tendency to learn and to act can be used to the best advantage, if the parents only know how. The Indians say that the mother is the first Guru; this should be realized by all parents. Education begins at home, and it is this first education which is the foundation of all that a child may learn in the future.

Health depends upon the music of one's life. When the mechanism of the body is regular in its rhythm and true in its tone, that is what is called health; and it is irregularity of rhythm and dissonance of tone which is called illness, and which physicians examine by counting the pulse, the beating of the heart, and by sounding the back and listening to the tone. They do these things in their capacity as physicians, not as musicians whose ears are trained to test the rhythm and tone.

The seer, the deep thinker, the knower of human nature, acts also as a musician by finding in people's actions their tone and rhythm. He notices in an untimely action, caused by ignorance or impatience, the irregularity of the rhythm; and in a word or action that has a harder or softer effect than it should have he sees the false tone, the false note. He also feels consonant or dissonant chords. When two people meet the dissonant chord of their evolution keeps them distant from one another in thought, although they may be sitting near together; and often a third person comes who either harmonizes the dissonant chord or produces disharmony in the consonant chord.

This shows that the whole of life is music. Wagner said, 'Who knows sound knows all things.' If music could be the foundation of the training of children, every life would be built on a good foundation. Life is rhythm and life is tone; and so is music. When a child learns music it learns the divine language; whatever be its work later in life if the child has intuition it will express in some way or other what has been the foundation of its character. It is not necessary for every child to be trained as a musician, for many musicians are not an ideal example to humanity, although in the East there was a time when kings chose musicians to be their companions. It was not that they enjoyed only their music, but also what was expressed in their lives, in their feelings, thought, manner, and action as an outcome of their constant contemplation of music. Also in the Western world the company of true musicians has always been an attraction.

Man is the fruit of the whole of creation, the source of which is absolute beauty. The purpose of creation is beauty. Nature in all its various aspects develops towards beauty, and therefore it is plain that the purpose of life is to evolve towards beauty. In giving education to children the first consideration should be that the seeds of beauty are sown in their hearts. When the plant grows it must be tenderly reared. The thriving of the plant is to the credit of the gardener; so the children's development is in the first instance to the credit of their parents.

The parents must themselves learn to be examples for their children. No theory has influence without practice. It is natural that parents, however taken up by the wickedness or folly of life, should wish their children to be different and better than themselves. But it is difficult; the child is impressionable and it develops that impression which it first received. Once the child sees in its parents a tendency towards drink or any other form of degeneration, it takes it for granted as it grows up that it must be the right or natural thing; for it says, 'If these things were not right my parents would not have done them'. In life the wrong thing attracts quickly, though the seeking of the soul is for what is right.

Parents are often anxious to collect wealth or property for their children; but there cannot be a greater wealth nor a better property than the impression they have left behind on the hearts of their children; the love and kindness they have spread in their circle of life multiplies in time, like the interest in the bank, and comes to the help of their children when they grow up in the form of love, kindness, and goodness from all sides.

The first education a child needs is to harmonize its thought, speech, and action. All things external have their reaction in one's inner life, and the inner has its reaction on the exterior. Therefore some knowledge of tone and rhythm is essential at the beginning of the child's education. A child should be taught the elements of music with regard to the pitch in which it should get in touch with its friends, with strangers, with its parents, while playing or at table; in every varying condition it should feel that the pitch is different. The child should be taught how to make its choice of words when speaking to different people, to strangers, to its friends, to its parents, to the servants in the house; making the voice softer or louder must be done with understanding.

The child is most energetic when it is growing, and every action, sitting, standing, walking, or running, every movement it makes, should be corrected and directed towards harmony and beauty. For the nature of life is intoxicating, and every action deepens the intoxication of life in a child, who is still ignorant of the outcome of every action; it knows little of the consequences and is only interested in the action. By nature a child is more enthusiastic and excitable than a grown-up person, and if its actions are not corrected or controlled it will mostly speak and act without consideration of harmony and beauty; for the nature of the child is like water which runs downwards and it needs a fountain to raise it upwards. Education is that fountain.

A child should be taught to speak and act according to the conditions prevailing at the moment: laughter at the time of laughter, seriousness at the moment when seriousness is required of it. In everything it does it must consider the conditions; it must watch for the opportunity to say and do the things it wishes.

For instance if a child makes a noise when the parents are at work or when friends are visiting them, if a child brings its complaints to its parents when it ought to be silent, if it cries or laughs at the wrong moment, it commits a fault against the law of rhythm. Rhythm is the consideration of time and condition, and this is most necessary. It is a great pity that at this present time, when the cry for freedom seems to be so dominant, people often think, 'Why should not the children have their freedom?' But it must be understood that it is not the path of freedom which leads to the goal of freedom. Liberty is not an ideal to begin life with, it is a stage of perfect freedom which must be kept in view in order to arrive at the desired end. Narrow is the way and strait is the gate, says the Bible of the road leading to the goal of freedom.

Next, a child must be taught to understand the beauty of word and action; which action is agreeable to itself and to others, and which is disagreeable; what word is pleasing and what word is displeasing. This is the true sight-reading and ear-training a child needs. It should be taught to sense its words and the words of others; whether they are graceful or devoid of grace. It must be able to recognize what action is beautiful, which manner is graceful; it must know and feel when its movements or manners are not up to the mark. In short it should be educated to be its own judge and to dislike what is ungraceful in itself; yet it should tolerate the lack of beautiful manner in others by realizing that it is itself subject to errors, and that annoyance on its part would in itself be bad manners.

If the child does not show interest in beauty it is only because something is closed in it. In every soul, however wicked it might seem, however stupid it might seem, beauty is hidden; and it is trust and confidence that will help us to draw out this beauty. However, the difficulty for everyone is to have patience. The lack of beauty in some people strikes us so hard that we lose patience because of it. In doing so we encourage them to become still worse; but if we could have the patience to endure and trust them, we could dig that beauty out; and some day we will, by the Fatherhood of God.

By trusting in the goodness of every person we will develop that beauty in ourselves. We do not, however, develop that beauty while thinking, 'I have it, but the other one has not!' but by forgetting ourselves and realizing that another person has got beauty in him although we do not always see it. And it is a weakness to turn our back upon anyone, child or grown-up, who seems to be lacking in the beauty that we expect. By opening ourselves to beauty we shall find it coming to life.

Consideration is the greatest of all virtues, for in consideration all virtues are born. Veneration for God, courtesy towards others, respect for those who deserve it, kindness to those who are weak and feeble, sympathy with those who need it, all these come from consideration.

All complaints that are made by friend about friend, or in the relations between husband and wife, master and servant, or between partners in business, show want of consideration. Everything man does which is called wrong, evil, or sin, is nothing but inconsiderateness. Consideration is a faculty which it is most necessary to develop in the child from the beginning; for once it has become inconsiderate, it is difficult to give it the sense of consideration. Consideration cannot be taught; it must come by itself; but the duty of the parents is to help it to rise in the child. They can very well accomplish this in a pleasant manner, without becoming a bore to the innocent mind of the child, by showing it where consideration is needed in different situations of life.

It is easy to accuse a child of inconsiderateness, but that does not always profit it. On the contrary, the child will often become annoyed at such accusations and hardened in its faults, defending its actions against the accusations of others, which is a natural human tendency. The way of the wise is to show appreciation whenever the child shows consideration, and to make it conscious of that virtue, so that it may be able to enjoy its beauty. This develops in the child a taste for virtue; it feels happy to act rightly, instead of always being forced to do so. It is on strength of mind that the entire life of the child depends, and strength of mind can be developed in the child by making it self-confident in all it thinks, says, or does; it must get to know something instead of being forced to believe it. Faith, which is taught as the most important lesson in many religions, does not necessarily mean faith in what another person says, thinks, or does, but in what one says, thinks, or does oneself. True faith is self-confidence. Every effort should be made to help the child to have confidence in itself. This can be done by removing from its nature confusion, indecision, and doubt, for these are the cause of all failure in life. Self-confidence and single-mindedness are the key to all success. The child should be encouraged to think or act not only because it is taught to do so, but because it knows already that it is right to think, speak, or act in a certain way; otherwise it will only be a machine which works without knowledge of the purpose or result of the work. The whole tragedy of life is that so many minds work mechanically like machines; only rarely some few act with knowledge, certainty, and self-confidence.

The child's mind is naturally more active than a grown-up person's, for two reasons. Firstly, the child's mind is growing with great energy, which makes it active during its growth. Furthermore, energy is active in its rise and loses power in its descent; it is for this reason that the child is restless in its thought and action. One child in the room can make one feel there are a hundred children. The child is never still, it delights in occupying its mental and physical energy in some way or other all the time.

It must be remembered that no time in man's life is so productive of action, both mental and physical, as childhood; but usually it happens that this most important period of the life of man is wasted in play which mostly brings no result. If this activity of mind and body which is exerted in play were used in educating the child without in the least straining its mind or body, it would be of great value in its life. But what we generally find in the world is quite the contrary. People say that early childhood is the time for a child to play. No doubt this is true; but it must be remembered that in every action, work or play, one spends a certain amount of energy; the difference is that work is what one is obliged to do and play what one does for one's pleasure.

But it is altogether a wrong principle, for children as well as for grown-ups, to divide work and play thus. Play should be useful and should be work at the same time; and work should be made like play, in order that it may not be a tedious task but a pleasure in life; if this idea were worked out well it would solve a great many labour problems which disturb the peace and order of humanity so much today.

It can best be done by teaching children to play and work at the same time, so that when they are grown-up work and play will continue to be the same. All that one does with pleasure is done well and produces a good effect. Doing depends upon the attitude of mind. When the mind is not in a good state, whatever be the work, however interesting, it will not be well done. To bring about peace and order in the world it is very necessary that all work should be made pleasant, and that all pleasure should be turned into work, so that in taking pleasure no work is lost and there is pleasure in working. The central theme in the education of children should be the occupying of every moment of their life in doing quite willingly something which is pleasurable and at the same time useful. Life is a great opportunity, and no moment of life should be lost.

The great fault of the modern system of education is that it only qualifies a man to obtain what he desires in life; and he tries to obtain this by every means, right or wrong, often with no regard for what losses or pain he causes others. The consequence of this is that life has become full of competition in trade, in the professions, and in the State. In order that one may gain another must surely lose. In this way the shadow changes its position from morning to evening; in the end the shadow must prove to be only a shadow, and one realizes it matters little which direction the shadow takes.

A child should begin to learn rivalry in goodness and competition in charity. Life is the outcome of reciprocity and reciprocity can be created by changing the attitude from a selfish to an unselfish one. The only hope of creating in the future a better spirit in the world, is to teach the ideal of unselfishness to the children, making this the spirit of the coming world.

The education of children should be considered from five different points of view: physical, mental, moral, social, and spiritual. If one side is developed and not the other sides, naturally the child will show some lack in its education.

There ought to be a standard of education for everyone in the country, rich or poor. It is the principal thing necessary for the order and peace of the community and the nation. No one, however poor his circumstances, should be deprived of education in his childhood, which is the only opportunity in life for a soul to acquire knowledge. It should be considered that every child is the child of the community. The idea that only the rich can afford to educate their children will not prove satisfactory in this epoch, for it shows the selfishness and negligence of one part of the community towards the other part. The neglected part must sooner or later rebel against it, as soon as they realize that they have been kept back by those with means, so that they cannot receive education and be prosperous in their lives. It is this revolt which has brought about a feeling of bitterness and indignation in the people; and this feeling will increase, to the great disadvantage of society, if not sufficient attention is given to public education.

The State is certainly responsible for the education of the people. It should be arranged that one and the same education is given to rich and poor alike in a course which consists of the five above-mentioned aspects of knowledge. Once that course is finished, then the children may take up any profession they like. If they want further education they may receive it from their private means if they can afford it, but the necessary education must be given to every child of the community. The course of education can certainly be compressed and made into a course of general education; the child should not only be taught to read and write but to have an all-round idea of life and how it can best be lived.

Physical education can be given, even from infancy, with the help of music. An infant should be made to move its hands and feet up and down, and as it grows it should be taught to do it rhythmically. When a child grows up, when it can dance and play different games, gymnastics should be taught, in such a way that the child may benefit by them but that they do not become a tedious work but a recreation.

Regularity is desirable in the building up of the personality of a child. It is habit which forms nature, but nature has no habit. It is always beneficial for a child to eat when hungry, to rest when tired. In this way the child makes its own nature instead of becoming subject to habits. Pure and nourishing food is necessary for a child while it grows. It needs all kinds of food to nourish its growth; also a child must have good long hours of sleep according to the needs of each child. At the same time a certain part of the day must be kept for the child to rest, and it must be done in such a manner that the child, whose natural tendency is to be active, may gladly take this rest. This can be done by telling it a story or giving it some work of art to look at, or by letting the child hear some music.

It is a popular belief that the childhood diseases most children go through are more or less inevitable. This is not so; they are caused by the artificiality of life.

A great deal of excitement, crying or laughing naturally upsets the rhythm of a child's body and mind. It is always wise to give the child, for its equilibrium, scope for action and reaction in everything it does. If a child is afraid of something, the best way to help it is to make it acquainted with the thing it is afraid of.

It is not advisable that the child should be taught always in the house, nor always at school. The study should be divided, partly indoors and partly outdoors. The teaching given to a child indoors should be different from the study given out of doors. The outdoor study should concern all that the child sees; one can then include the practice or the experience of what it has learned indoors. In short, a child's health must be considered as part of its education; study and health go together.

Together with physical culture, mental training is very necessary for a child. There are two things which ought to be remembered: one is to develop the mental power of the child, the other to give fineness to a child's mentality. Very often the development in a certain direction hinders the progress in some other direction. In the first place, to make its mentality strong, the child should be taught to concentrate its mind through study and play. It should be given some enterprise which takes most of its attention in one direction, making the child single-minded.

The child must be kept from excitement or passion of any kind, for it is tranquillity of mind which gives a child strength, balance, self-control, self-confidence, and determination. It also strengthens the child's mentality, and it is certainly on the strength of the mentality that success in life chiefly depends. But strong mentality does not suffice for every purpose of life; besides strength, fineness is necessary. In order to develop this fineness in a child, every help must be given to sharpen its wits. Wit needs an opportunity to develop and that opportunity can be given by training a child to grasp things. A certain amount of encouragement can also be given to stimulate its wits. A child must be helped to perceive keenly what time is suitable for a certain action, what it can say or do at one time and what it should not say and do at another time. Great care should be taken in teaching good manners to a child, so that in time it may become natural to show in its manner the beauty hidden in its soul. Fine mentality can be seen in keen perception, in love of subtlety, and in the gracefulness and refinement of manner which complete mental culture.

Moral education depends upon three things: the right direction of love, a keen sense of harmony, and the proper understanding of beauty. The child should be taught to make the right use of its emotional and sentimental faculties; and the right use is to show its charity of heart in generous actions, and first to its immediate surroundings. The child must learn that love means sacrifice; also it must know that love is best expressed in service of any kind; that emotion is best used in kind action, and sentiment in creating harmony. A child must understand that love should be shown by being considerate, and its sentiment must teach it respect and consideration for others.

A child is a growing plant and it needs not only bodily nourishment, but also the nourishment of the heart; and that is best taught by loving the child and by reciprocating its love. And yet it must be taught balance, to keep its emotion within certain bounds and limitations. A child must be taught the use of love through the expression of sweetness in its thought, speech, and action. A wrongly given love spoils the child by making it rude, vain, and indifferent. One must not show all one's love to one's children, especially not in any emotional form. One must have a certain amount of reserve in one's own self, for the child to take example by and to follow. An excessive amount of reserve may imply want of love, which is fruitless at times; a balance of love and reserve in dealing with a child is the right thing.

It is very important to cultivate the spirit of generosity in the child's heart. Generosity does not necessarily mean extravagance or lack of consideration for things one possesses. The real spirit of generosity is best expressed in charity of heart. Obeying, respecting, serving, learning, responding, all this comes from charity of heart, and it grows by developing generosity of nature.

One must protect the child against the inclination to be led astray by others, for a generous child is often subject to misleading influences. Also it must be kept from being generous with other people's things, even with the possessions of its own parents. Generosity on the part of a child is only the opening of the heart. When the heart of a child is closed, the child is deprived of expression; and when once it has started in this way its entire life develops on the same lines. It is the generosity of the heart which is the mystery of genius, for to give expression to art or science, poetry or music, the heart must be opened first; and this can only be accomplished by the generosity of the heart. Tolerance, forgiveness, endurance, fortitude, are all the outcome of this virtue.

A friendly spirit is the natural spirit of the soul. Nothing in the child should be encouraged which forms an obstacle to its friendly tendency; but it is the responsibility of the parents to watch with whom the child wants to be friends, and to keep the child always in the company of desirable children. The guardian must not make the child feel that it is deprived of the choice of its friends, but it should be guided in order to keep it among desirable friends.

The freedom of the child must always be considered; it should never be forced but only guided gently. One should produce in a child the desire to choose as its friends those whom it feels to be congenial. As soon as the liberty of a child is interfered with, the child begins to feel itself a captive and the lantern of its conscience becomes dim. Therefore the duty of the parents is to guide the child constantly, yet freeing it gradually to make a choice in everything in life. Parents who do not understand this and do not attach sufficient importance to it, very often cause the child to go astray while trying to guide it.

A child should learn to recognize its relation and duty to all those around it. One should let it know what is expected of it by its father, mother, brothers, and sisters; for the recognition of relationship is the sign of human character which is not seen among animals. A son who has not been a good son to his mother will not be a good husband to his wife, for he has missed his first chance of developing thoughtfulness and the love quality. But as the child grows it must be led to have some idea of the further relationship between human beings. For the world is a family, and the right attitude of a young soul must be to see in every man his brother and in every woman his sister; he must look on aged people as he would on his father or mother.

The betterment of the world mostly depends upon the development of the coming generation. The ideal of human brotherhood should be taught at home; this does not mean that the child must recognize human brotherhood before recognizing the relationship with his own brothers and sisters; but the relationship at home must be the first lesson in human brotherhood which the child may reach by realizing the brotherhood of the nation, of the race, and then of the world. It is a fault when a person does not progress in the path of brotherhood. The child should be taught to picture first its own town as a family, then its nation as a family, and then the entire continent as a family, in order to arrive at the idea that the whole world is a family.

A child should know the moral of give and take; it must know that it should give to others what it wishes to receive from them. The great fault of humanity today is that everyone seeks to get the better of others, by which one is often caught in one's own net. Fair dealing in business and in a profession and the honouring of one's word are most necessary today. It is the spirit of brotherhood which will solve the problems of business and professions, as of education and politics, which are so difficult to solve at present owing to the absence of brotherly feeling.

The education of the younger generation needs the spiritual ideal more than anything else. Since the world has become so materialistic man has almost lost sight of the main object of life, which is the spiritual ideal. Spiritual ideal does not mean that children should necessarily be attached to any particular faith, or that any particular Church should be forced upon them. What is needed is simply to give some ideal to the child to look forward to, some high ideal, yet one which the child's mind can conceive. The divine ideal has been given to mankind for spiritual attainment in all periods of the world's history, and humanity will never outgrow that ideal.

Whatever be the stage of human progress, the divine ideal will be the only ideal which will help both old and young to steer their way through the sea of life. It is the loss of divine ideal which causes the breakdown in the life of individuals and of humanity in general; the cause of paralysis in modern progress is no other than the loss of divine ideal. Man, revolting against existing religion or religious authority, has naturally forgotten the divine ideal, which is really the one yearning of his soul. A time has come when man has neither his ancestors' religion nor a religion of his own.

A child must learn that there is some ideal; that towards that ideal the whole of humanity is unconsciously or consciously progressing. The child must know that it is responsible for all it does, not only to its fellow-men, but to someone who watches it constantly and from whom nothing can be hidden; that however much justice may seem to be suffering in the world, there is somewhere the balance of justice which in time must balance things; and that death is only a bridge by which the soul passes from one sphere to another. The child which respects age, which is considerate for the elderly in its surroundings, and which imagines them to be an ideal that is to be followed, shows it has religion in itself.

Spiritual ideal is the natural inclination of every soul. It needs no great effort to guide a child towards spirituality; it is more difficult to keep a child from it, which many parents do today who are anxious about their child being drawn towards spiritual ideals. No doubt, too much religion is not good for a child; it makes the child fixed in its ideas, and takes away the liquidity that every soul naturally possesses. Giving the child ideas of spirits or ghosts or of heaven and hell is not desirable. The child's imagination should be kept within the range of its reasoning, and yet reason must not be made an obstacle in the way of the child's imagination. For very often the child's imagination goes further than that of its parents, and it would be cruel to hinder it by limiting the child to one's own religious and material ideas. The principal thing in spirituality is genuineness of life; in other words: sincerity. The child must be taught to say what it means. If it is by nature artistic in its expression, which is often seen in exceptionally intelligent children, then the child must be kept close to reality, in order that it may not be led astray by the art of its intelligent expression.

Before the child goes to bed, it should be taught, in some form or other, to think gratefully of the One from whom all goodness comes and to whom all is known. The child may also be taught to wish good to all in the name of the One who has created all. What a child should wish for its parents or for others is good health, long life, right guidance from above, prosperity, success, happiness, and love.

6
The Training of Youth

YOUTH for every soul is the season of blossoming, and it can be divided into three stages: early youth, the middle part of youth, and the last stage of youth.

There is great difficulty in the training of youth, because in youth a child becomes less receptive. The child is passive and therefore easy to guide, but youth is the time of rising energy, both physical and mental; therefore youth is expressive, and what is expressive cannot be receptive at the same time. Parents make a great mistake when they continue the same method with a youth which they applied in his childhood. There is the time of ploughing, there is the time of sowing, and there is the time of reaping the harvest; it is not all done at the same time.

In youth a child is most susceptible to influences, and at the same time most repellent of influences which fall beneath its standard. The child which has believed and obeyed its parents in its childhood does not necessarily believe and obey them during the time of its youth. The parents must realize this and change their manner of correcting and guiding the child from the beginning of its youth.

Youth makes the child inclined to look on its parents or guardians as old-fashioned people. The present education given in schools and the child's own experience of things around it support it in this idea. If the parents force their ideas on the youth, he first plays with them, making them think that he agrees with them; but in the next stage he avoids them, and in the third stage he argues with them and opposes them. Once a youth has arrived at this third stage he stands on his own feet, and there is little hope that the parents can guide him; they are then obliged to let him take his own way whether right or wrong.

Among a hundred youths one may take a right way by himself, and five out of the hundred may find their way through the dark but ninety-five are lost owing to the absence of guidance. Life is a sea upon which it is difficult to find one's way, and as direction is necessary when travelling on the sea, so guidance is most necessary during the period of youth.

The principal thing one has to remember concerning the education of young people is to help them, without their knowing it, to think for themselves. The nature of youth, and especially that of the youth of today, is such that as soon as he feels that he is directed by someone he feels that he is harnessed to a carriage, and in this he feels the absence of freedom. An essential thing in guiding the youth is to make lines of thought and to place them before him, in order that he may use the lines as a track to follow. True virtue comes from independent thinking, not from being under subjection. But at the same time it must be remembered that the independent spirit which is expressed without consideration is devoid of beauty. It is desirable that a youth should show consideration in his thought, speech, and action, for freedom without consideration lacks beauty.

In the guidance of youth the same five directions of development must be considered as in the education of children: physical, mental, moral, social, and spiritual.

While considering the physical development of a youth one should remember that youth is the time of full blossom, the most delicate and important time in everyone's life. If the blossom is ruined the fruit is lost. Therefore youth is the golden opportunity.

It is the time when a person is not yet set in his ideas, not addicted to certain habits, ready to accept new ideas. An intellectual youth generally seeks for new ideas. Youth is a time when one is most inclined to changes of every sort, and therefore youth is not fixed in particular habits.

Very often the parents, not knowing what it involves when their child grows too rapidly, do not consider many things concerning its life which may harm it later. It is essential that special attention be given to the balance between activity and repose, to the sleep, food, and recreation of the youth. In a child a nervous temperament is a sign of intelligence; a genius is generally nervous in his youth.

Youth is the time when, if the child is sensitive to conditions, every little thing around it will go to its heart. If there is disharmony around a youth, if there is sorrow, disagreement among his people, depression, it all weighs upon him, at a time when he is capable of feeling and yet incapable of helping the situation. It is not fair to draw sympathy from the youth, and especially from the one who has a feeling heart, for one's pains and troubles; for there is a time for every experience and that time comes later. If pain is sown in the heart of the youth decay develops at the root of his life, making him bitter all through life.

Wise parents or guardians must know that youth is the springtime of every soul, the kingliness which is given once to every soul to experience. No soul may be debarred from nature's kingdom. It is the duty of parents and guardians to respect youth and take care that this springtime is given free to the youth, without burdening his life with the woes of worldly life which await every soul.

What is called youth in general terms is particularly the springtime of the physical body; and therefore if the child is physically well nourished and well drilled, so that he shows power and energy in every movement, it makes him fit for any sort of work that he may desire to learn, and for making his way in life. Seeing the youth enthusiastic and vigorous, the parents sometimes do not consider the fact that every burden, physical or mental, which might weigh him down is most injurious at this period of his life, although at a later age the same burden would not be so harmful. Youth being the time of full bloom, if the child does not show abundant energy and enthusiasm then at what other time will it do so? Therefore it is necessary that by physical exercise, proper rest, and good nourishment the youth is kept in perfect balance.

In youth an extra energy is born which expresses itself in passion and emotion; if the parents do not know how to deal with it the child can easily abuse it. There is no end of abuse of energy to be found in the world today in spite of all the attention that seems to be awakening in various educational centres. The idea is that it is no use watching a child, for this shows lack of trust; nor is it right to correct a child when it has gone too far in a certain playful tendency. There is no end of temptation which attracts a youth. It is natural for a youth who has just passed his period of playfulness to continue to play in the ways which to him seem harmless. An important part of the education of a youth is therefore to be told things plainly, and to be made aware of the advantages and disadvantages of various interests in life. It is not much use for a child to read books concerning the life of youth. Personal advice on the subjects in question will prove to be more effective.

Very often, before the parents could ever imagine their child's inclination towards things of a serious nature, the child happens to have already experienced them, while being absolutely ignorant of the consequences. The younger generation seems to be declining every day in physical health, in enthusiasm, compared with the people of the past. So it is most necessary that in the present age special care should be taken to ensure that youth is trained to realize the great importance in life of good physical health, upon which depend happiness, prosperity, and success.

Mental strength in youth depends upon single-mindedness, and youth is inclined to look in a thousand directions instead of keeping its mind fixed on one object at a time. A youth who is helped, or who is naturally inclined, to keep his mind in one single direction without wavering, is sure to have success in life.

Youth also has an inclination to be impatient, for it is the time when energy is working with great force, and this makes youth impulsive and lacking in patience. But if the child were taught patience when it is not already inclined to it by nature, it would surely succeed in all that it might undertake in life.

The time of youth has a certain influence on the life of the child, in that it makes its mind too active; and too much activity produces confusion in its life. Besides the physical energy beating constantly through the pulse of the youth brings about difficulties in his life. Therefore guardians who are eager for his studies and progress should take care of the mind of the youth, which needs to be clear, poised, and balanced; without this the child is a trouble to his parents and a difficulty for himself. Youth with thought and consideration is like a flower with a beautiful colour and fragrance.

The moral education of the youth is also of the greatest importance. A child must grow to recognize a father in every elderly man, a mother in every elderly woman, a sister in girls of his age, and a brother in boys like himself. In this way the obligations of one soul to another in this world will be better understood. When a youth considers his duty only to someone closely related to him, and not to the others, he becomes limited; his point of view becomes narrowed. How much better the world would be if every young man considered it his duty to take care of and be responsible for every young girl as he would for his own sister; there would not be so much sorrow and disappointment. The greatest moral a youth could be taught is to understand his obligations to others, in order to fill his place fittingly in the scheme of life.

Youth should be taught to recognize the great power of honesty, instead of considering honesty only as a virtue. The child must be taught to make an ideal for itself and to live up to it. It is no use giving an ideal to a child, for the ideal of one person is not made for another.

A young man who realizes that his word engages his honour is an example for the present age when the word, even supported by twenty seals and stamps and a signature on a paper, does not hold good. A youth with this sense of honour and dignity, whose heart is awakened to human sympathy, who has a keen sense of duty and who shows thought and consideration for others, is a model for the present generation in moulding its personality.

Moral development does not consist only of acquiring an ideal and good manners, but also of the power to endure all the jarring influences that one meets in everyday life. Besides the consciousness of one's obligations towards everyone that one meets in life is an elementary part of moral education. A youth can be without regard for delicacy of thought, but if his morality is developed he will act morally with greater ease than those who have learned morals later in life.

Life is nature, time makes it; once a person becomes hardened in a certain way his soul becomes a mould of that particular nature, and all he says or does in life shows the design of this mould.

Very often it happens that a person arrives at the realization of the great value of moral qualities in the later part of his life, and yet cannot act according to the ideal he values most. It is just like an earthen pot which, having been put into the mould before it was properly finished, comes out of the fire hardened; the potter may want to change the shape of the pot, but it cannot be done any more. If parents and guardians only realized what an opportunity the time of youth is in life, they would make out of youth what the Indians call the 'plant of wishes', which bears as its fruit all one's desires.

In youth there is hope, and there is an object to look forward to. In accomplishing this object a youth requires two powers: the power of will and the power of the beauty of thought, speech, and action. Many people in this world, with all their power, physical, mental, and every other form of power, even with an army at their disposal, prove helpless through the lack of beauty, the power of which is sometimes greater than any other. It is the balance of will and beauty that results in wisdom; and in a youth these three qualities form a trinity, which is the ideal of perfection.

Youth is naturally inclined to be sociable. If it is not so it means something is wrong, for it is most desirable for a youth to make friends and to show reciprocity in friendship, in love, or in courtship, and to show courtesy, kindness, and goodwill. Joining youth associations, looking after one's friends and relatives, giving them welcome and warmth, is something that is expected of the youth. There is, however, always a danger for the youth who is sociable and mixes freely in all circles whether desirable or undesirable. Youth is to some extent a time of blindness, when the passions and emotions are in full play. It is just as easy for a youth to take a wrong direction, as it is for him to take a right direction; and a growing youth, full of enthusiasm, overcome with emotion, and eager to experience anything new and interesting, may take any road in life opened to him by his friends. Therefore it is the duty of the guardians to keep him away from all undesirable influences, without giving the slightest idea that they control him and his affairs or deprive him of his freedom.

The higher the ideal of the youth, the greater is the future for him. A youth who is led to work for friends of his age, for his associations, for his community, for the nation, is indeed on the right road.

The youth who avoids the friendship of his own sex, or the one who is not attracted by the opposite sex, is abnormal, and either of these cases should be taken as a disorder and should be treated in its early stages. If it is allowed to go on it results in great disappointment. The youth who is disinclined to associate with his own sex is as a rule a timid nature and weak in will-power. It is sometimes caused by feebleness of body and sometimes by having been brought up with extra love, care, and tenderness at the hands of women alone. Therefore the life of a boy should begin with having boys as companions. In this way he receives from others the nature which is necessary for him.

It is one thing to be born male; it is another thing to develop a male personality. It is not sufficient to be born male; a male personality must be developed. It can be developed in youth, but if this time is missed, then it is almost too late, although no doubt a youth of such an abnormal nature can still be placed in surroundings from which in time he may receive the impressions he needs to complete his male personality.

A youth who responds to joy and to sorrow and to those near and dear to him, who echoes every impulse, who is interested in everything desirable and who is alive to all pleasure and joy, is a normal youth. If he is guided rightly he will make his life worth living.

The same tendencies may be observed in girls. A girl who is not brought up with other girls develops a character which is not feminine. The consequences are she is repulsive to her own sex and unattractive to the opposite sex. When in youth a girl begins to show male traits in her personality, she should by every means be placed in female surroundings, which in time may so impress her spirit that her personality partakes of the qualities that are necessary to complete her female personality.

There are also youths who are strongly drawn to their own sex and away from the opposite sex. Amongst them some are physically and some mentally abnormal; but there are some in whom the desire for the opposite sex is still asleep, and it needs awakening; very often in cases of the latter kind difficulties arise. People blame them for something which is not their fault; for people not knowing the truth expect them to be as responsive to the opposite sex as everybody else. And when they do not find them as they expect them to be people become impatient with them. Many courtships and marriages are destroyed by this lack of understanding. If one only knew the art of doing it one would wait and help gently and patiently, as if for the ripening of green fruit.

A youth with good manners and education yet without endurance, cannot make great progress in life, for he tends only to associate with those who come up to his standard; he will ignore or avoid those who fall beneath it; and as his sense of discernment becomes keener he will become more and more intolerant.

The downfall of modern civilization is caused by the lack of sincere sociability. There is a diplomatic form of politeness which is only politeness in form, without sincerity; but true politeness belongs to the one who is sympathetic. Sincerity is the principal thing in life.

Youth is the age which is most attracted to superficiality; that is the reason why many youths adopt an artificial manner of thought, speech, and action, which is very undesirable and does not benefit their life.

It is important to inculcate sincerity in the character of the youth. To give a youth a love of sincerity is extremely useful, for the power of sincerity can work miracles. Also pride, a natural spirit which grows in a youth, must be moulded into an ideal. The same pride which makes man stiff, stern, and inconsiderate, if developed into what is called self-respect, will be the true sign of honour in life; for pride when guided into the right channel gives rise to consideration. Such a person becomes careful not to think, say, or do what falls beneath his standard of virtue. Pride rightly directed moulds the character, and it is the perfected character which culminates in an ideal.

The development of the spiritual side of the youth comes before anything else in life. Often spirituality is confused with religion; in reality, however, this word has quite a different meaning. Religion for many is that which they know to be their people's belief; spirituality is the revealing of the divine light which is hidden in every soul. It has no concern with any particular religion. Whatever religion a person belongs to is no good to him if he has no spirituality. But if a man is spiritual, then whatever be his faith he will profit by it. Therefore, before thinking what religion the youth should belong to, one should train him in a spiritual ideal.

A youth of today, trained in the spirit of commercialism and with material motives put before him, can never grow up to become a really happy person who can impart his happiness to his fellow-men. The greatest drawback of modern times is the bringing up of a youth in an absolutely material atmosphere, so that he has nothing to look forward to beyond matter and material conditions, which are as poor as matter itself. No child comes on earth without a spiritual ideal, but it is the surroundings in which it lives, its guardians, its associates, that make the child materialistic. It cannot develop by itself when all the surroundings are different. In this way the spiritual ideal which the child brings on earth is strangled by material guardians and associates.

The world of today would have been much better than it is if there had been a spiritual ideal placed before it as well as a material ideal, which seems to be the only goal of the modern world. If one can learn from experience, the recent catastrophes have not been a small example of what the development of materialism can bring about. If the world goes on in the same manner, what will be the result? There is no hope for the betterment of humanity until the spiritual ideal has been brought forward and made the central theme of education both at home and in the schools. This only can be the solution of the difficult problem of world reform that faces humanity.

How to begin the training of youth in spiritual ideals is not an easy problem to solve; for there are several dangers which have to be considered before beginning such a training with a youth. It is not necessary that the youth should be made a religious fanatic or religiously proud; he must not be made to think that his spiritual direction makes him superior to others. Goodness always gives a certain vanity, and an undeveloped spirituality brings a still greater vanity. If by spirituality a youth is made bigoted in his own faith, looking at the followers of every other faith with contempt, or with a sort of indifference, it cannot be right. How many religious souls there still are in this world who think their scripture is the only scripture, their Church the only religion, and everyone else infidels! Such a faith can never produce spirituality in a soul.

Spirituality comes from the softening of the heart, which becomes frozen by the coldness of the surrounding life. The influence of worldly life upon the mind generally has a freezing effect; for selfishness coming from all sides naturally makes a man cool and selfish. Therefore it is the constant softening of the heart of the youth that is necessary. There are two ways of softening the heart; one is by helping the youth to open himself to the beauty which is shining in all its various forms. The other is to give him a tendency to righteousness, which is the very essence of the soul. These things cannot be taught, but they can be awakened in the heart of the youth if the parents or the guardians only know how.

The child must not be forced by principles, but love of virtue should be created in his heart, for in the inner nature of every soul there is love of virtue. Spirituality in the real sense of the word is the discovering of the spirit, which is attained by rising above self or by diving into self.

The greatest fault of the day is the absence of stillness. Stillness is nowadays often taken as leisureliness or as slowness. Modern man lacks concentration and carries with him an atmosphere of restlessness; with all his knowledge and progress he feels uncomfortable himself, and unintentionally brings discomfort to others. Stillness is therefore the most important lesson that can be taught to the youth of today.

Spirituality is like the water hidden in the depth of the earth: hidden in the heart of man, this water which is spirituality must be, so to speak, dug out. This digging is done when one takes pains in awakening one's sympathy towards others, in harmonizing with others and in understanding others.

The outer knowledge of human life and nature is called philosophy, but the inner knowledge of these is called psychology. This knowledge can be studied; yet the real spirit of this knowledge is manifested in the awakening of the soul. The youth must be given higher thoughts in order that he may think about a higher ideal, uphold a higher conception of life, gain a higher aspiration, and carry through life a higher attitude, a higher point of view.

It is in the ennobling of the soul that spirituality lies, not in a mere show of spirituality; and nobleness of the soul is realized in the feeling of selflessness. Whatever be a man's rank or position, if he shows selflessness in life he is truly noble. The spiritual nobility is the real aristocracy, for it expresses itself in democracy. In a really spiritual person aristocracy and democracy are one, for these ideals, which both have their spiritual beauty, are summed up in the one spirit of nobleness. A youth must be taught that it is not becoming angelic which shows spirituality; it is becoming human which is the true sign of the spiritual man.